PRAYER
for the day

Selections from the
BBC Radio 4 programme

Compiled by Hope Sealy

BBC BOOKS

ACKNOWLEDGEMENTS

Our thanks are due to the following for their kind permission to reproduce their work:

Faber and Faber Ltd: 'Markings' by Dag Hammarskjöld translated by W. H. Auden and Leif Sjoberg (p. 24); Janet Morley: prayer from *All Desires Known* published by Women in Theology and the Movement for the Ordination of Women, 1988 (p. 40); William Collins Sons and Co Ltd: 'Poustinia' by Catherine de Hueck Doherty, 1975 (p. 47); Jesuit Missions: passage based on extract from 'The Jesuit Refugee Service: A Vision' in *Jesuits and Friends* (p. 49); Anthony Sheil Associates Ltd: 'The Desert' by M. Louise Haskins, Hodder & Stoughton Ltd (p. 52); Concordia Publishing House, USA: prayer by Alfred Doerffler (p. 53); Quest Publishing House, USA: 'Last Song; from *I Send a Voice* by Evelyn Eaton, 1978 (p. 57); Oxford University Press: 'God's Life Within' by Tukarum from *The Oxford Book of Prayer* (p. 67); Revd J. E. Cotter: prayer from *Prayer in the Day*, Cairns Publications, 1986 (p. 77); Victor Gollancz Ltd: prayer from *God of a Hundred Names*, compiled by Barbara Green and Victor Gollancz (p. 79)

The publishers and author have made every attempt to contact copyright holders for the use of the material in this book but, if copyright material has been used inadvertently without permission, the publishers would be delighted to hear from those concerned.

Published by BBC Books,
A division of BBC Enterprises Ltd
Woodlands, 80 Wood Lane, London W12 0TT

First published 1989
Reprinted 1989 (twice)
© the contributors 1989
ISBN 0 563 20732 9

Typeset in 10/11½ pt Garamond
by Wilmaset, Birkenhead, Wirral
Printed and bound in Great Britain by Redwood Burn Ltd, Trowbridge, Wiltshire
Cover printed by Fletchers of Norwich

FOREWORD

By David Winter, Head of Religious Broadcasting, BBC

The brief religious spots in BBC Radio's output are familiar friends to its listeners. People get up to them, burn their toast to them and catch their trains to them. They are part of the broadcasting landscape.

Among them, at an early hour on Radio 4, is *Prayer for the Day*. From Monday to Friday this consists of a scripted talk, with music, introduced by a reading from the Bible and culminating in a prayer – hence its title. On Saturdays it has, for a couple of years, taken a different form: well-known guests have been interviewed about their own experience and perception of faith, and each guest has rounded the programme off with a prayer of his or her own choice or composition.

Like most successful radio formats, this one sounds very simple: deceptively so. In fact, finding the right guest, asking the right questions and arriving at a conclusion demands great skill and sensitivity on the part of the presenter. For most of the time this presenter has been Hope Sealy, and it is encouraging now to find some of these Saturday reflections given a less transient presentation than a brief radio item can possibly allow.

Certainly brevity has not meant superficiality, as these transcripts demonstrate. Many of Hope Sealy's contributors have spoken with remarkable honesty and insight. There is little here of the preacher, but much of the searcher. Those who speak mirror the anxieties, longings and hopes for many who listen.

Radio scripts do not always translate well into print – but an honest, genuine and even painful quest for faith and meaning transcends the limitations of any medium. I hope this book will recall for many readers who know *Prayer for the Day* the moments when it has spoken to them and for them. I also hope it may encourage readers who have never heard the programme to switch on Radio 4 at ten to seven on Saturday mornings!

INTRODUCTION

For the past two years I've had the pleasure of meeting and talking with a wide cross-section of people for Radio Four's Saturday *Prayer for the Day* programme. My brief was to speak to my guest about a prayer or passage or verse which had made a deep impact on his or her spiritual life.

Most of the interviews were done in the homes or offices of my guests. Sometimes we sat outside in the garden, birdsong making an acceptable background to our conversation. At other times we crouched in bedrooms, to get away from various mechanical or human sounds elsewhere in the house.

When I arrived, recorder over my shoulder, my guest usually knew the prayer or verse to be discussed, but there were times when we sat for quite a while discussing a sort of short list of verses or prayers before deciding on the 'winner'.

Always there was welcome, warmth and a sense of fun. Always there was fresh insight into both the prayer and the guest.

I hope that you will get a sense of warmth from the conversations quoted in this book and that you'll enjoy having the prayers and verses presented in this way.

My thanks to my producer, Caroline Donne, for giving me the opportunity to present this programme. My thanks to those who participated in the programme for their contribution and for their permission to be quoted in this book.

Hope Sealy

SISTER LAVINIA BYRNE, of the Institute of the Blessed Virgin Mary, Co-editor of *The Way*, a quarterly publication on contemporary Christian spirituality

On her chosen prayer

The God in this particular psalm, Psalm 144, is a God who's full of power and energy. But the reason I like praying with this psalm is that the God in it is a God who wants to share power and creativity and energy with us.

I first used this psalm to pray with when I was staying in France, in the Dordogne. I'd gone there to make a retreat, to spend some time praying alone. It's a part of France where there are lots of rocks, lots of hydro-electric works, things that you don't actually meet in central London, and I found it thrilling to see evidence of the energy of God in creation and to see a God who wants to share this energy with us.

The psalm speaks about battles and wars and I believe we do have to take up arms. I don't mean literally, that we physically have to go out and fight people, but we have to be prepared to use power and to use creativity. We mustn't pretend that we don't have any power, any creativity. It's a terribly tempting option for Christians, to say, 'We have no power. We're powerless.' I believe that if we acknowledge we have power, we begin to use it responsibly and we actually can do something against evil by standing up for what is right.

It's very difficult discerning what is right and what is wrong in all the options that are open to us, but I believe that if we listen to the voice that comes from within the citadel, from within the place where God is strong, we will know what we should do. I believe the temptation for us is not to listen to what God is saying within, not to listen to the messages that come from the fortress.

If we are individual little fortresses, if we are little rocks, and if we are little strongholds, this is so that although we're empowered from within, our presence in the world can be a transforming presence. Very often, as Christian people, we've been so thrilled to be accepted by society that we've chosen the option of conformity and establishment rather than what is possibly a more Christian option, which is the option of dissent . . . The option of being a people who ask questions and who aren't satisfied with some of the answers that are provided, satisfied by our desire to be successful and to be accepted. Perhaps being a Christian is about being uncomfortable.

I also find it very impressive that this psalm is for everybody. It's not saying that men are powerful and women aren't, or that women are powerful and men aren't. It's giving the responsibility to all of us.

From Psalm 144

Blessed be the Lord, my rock,
who trains my hands for war,
and my fingers for battle;
my rock and my fortress,
my stronghold and my deliverer,
my shield and the one in whom I take refuge. . . .
Bow thy heavens, O Lord, and come down!
Touch the mountains that they smoke!
Flash forth thy lightning and scatter them,
Send out thy arrows and rout them!

●

TREVOR HALL, Race Relations Consultant at the Home Office. Born in Barbados, he came to Britain in the 1960s

On his optimism
I would say that the strength that I have as a black individual in Britain today has come from my family background in Barbados and from my church background. In Barbados it is the norm to be a churchgoer and a Christian person and that has always strengthened me to face life's challenges as they come.

On his choice of prayer
In Barbados I was a very strong member of the local Church Lads' Brigade and their motto is 'Fight the Good Fight', so this hymn has meant a lot to me. What it said to me was that I should see life as a challenge and I was to be prepared to face up to this challenge. I would see myself to be a Christian who is trying to live a good life, rather than a Christian who is just involved in being good.

I'm very concerned in my particular job in looking at how people from the various ethnic communities are perceived in this country. I'm equally concerned about what I call the 'unheard voices' in our inner cities. I feel it's important if I'm going to be identified with Christian witness to stand up occasionally and to be heard. I believe the Christian person can no longer expect not to be controversial. I believe when we look at the disadvantages that people meet in terms of how systems and organisations perceive them, that as Christians we need to challenge whether this is God-fairness. I don't think it is God-fairness to say that because you have a difference that you should accept discrimination of any kind.

This prayer takes me back to the fact that one has to fight these systems, one has to fight these inadequacies, one has to fight these prejudices. I do believe there is a promised land. I believe that everything that one does and one is doing as a Christian person must lead towards a land that is beautiful, a land of honey and milk.

I see a land in which difference does not create deficits for people; a land in which God's creation, human beings, are respected for the fact that they are God's creation; a land in which men and women, black and white, rich and poor, will feel that they are equal in the creation of God.

Fight the Good Fight
J. S. B. Monsell (1811–75)

Fight the good fight with all thy might,
Christ is thy strength, and Christ thy right;
Lay hold on life, and it shall be
Thy joy and crown eternally.

•

JOHN HEATH-STUBBS, poet

On his chosen meditation

The thing to me that's most powerful in the verse is the paradox that God might need our forgiveness. It's a thought which some people might find very disturbing, but which I think might lurk at the back of a lot of people's minds. It is only the God who became man and who is crucified for us that we can

7

forgive, and who has the right to forgive us. The incarnation is a very real thing for me. God without the whole full Trinitarian doctrine is just a windy abstraction.

I have difficulty with the man Jesus, with the human Jesus; but the idea of a God who is something eternally giving himself, that this is the whole creative act, this is very real to me. The whole creation was an act of self-giving.

I can't say that personally I've ever felt a need to forgive God, but I'm sometimes weighed down by the amount of suffering and evil in the world. I'm blind, but I don't hold my blindness against God. Ninety per cent of the time I'm not aware that I'm blind. I have such a strong imagination that I have to remind myself very often that I haven't seen things. For instance, if I go to the theatre with somebody and they just hint at what the sets and the costumes are like, I think afterwards that I've seen them.

The lines also speak of God creating the snake in Paradise. This is a paradox that's occupied a lot of people. Charles Williams who influenced me a lot said that he did not ask to be tempted. 'Ultimately,' he said, 'almost until the very end, the universe has to seem unfair. We did not ask to be tempted.' But of course we can accept this when we know we are redeemed.

Because I think freedom goes very deep into creation, and freedom does mean the possibility of forsaking God, God cannot force us to be loved. I don't agree with Einstein that God does not throw dice. I think God threw dice from the start, giving to his inanimate as well as to his animate creation thereby certain freedom to evolve, to evolve sometimes in ways which are very disturbing and paradoxical to us.

Paradise is to me a timeless sort of innocence which we can sometimes enter, it's what people partly enter in states of vision like Wordsworth or Blake entered. Sometimes, just sometimes, I've felt aware of this Paradise.

From the *Rubáiyát of Omar Khayyám*
Freely translated by Edward Fitzgerald (1809–83)

O thou, who man of baser earth did make
And even with paradise did devise the snake,
For all the sin the face of wretched man is black with
Man's forgiveness give and take.

SISTER MARTINA, OP, a Dominican sister from St Michael's convent, Hertfordshire

On God as reflected in the psalms

It's a big God. There's an American poem which begins, 'Our God's a Big God', and it's that kind of God that's reflected in the psalms. Sometimes, of course, he gets quite petty and vindictive. Sometimes I suppose those bits appeal to me, but on the whole I tend to leave them out.

On her chosen psalm

I think that it's the whole attitude of God that I love in this psalm. God is in me, is in our lives, permeates the universe. The God in this psalm is the ground of my being. This attitude of God just speaks to me.

I also think it's a wonderful psalm because it has so many elements of prayer in it. It's full of praise, it's full of awe, it's full of adoration, thanksgiving, petition. It's got all the elements of prayer right there and they just flow out. It's like something coming out of a very full heart. It touches some part of me that very often ordinary prayers don't touch. It reaches a depth of my being; it's like God, the ground of my being, and it's a way of expressing my faith which I feel really comfortable with.

I think the thing that really touches me is that I am in God and God is in me. I'm held in God, whatever's happening and wherever I am; whether I'm asleep or awake, or talking or being quiet, or whatever I'm doing, God is in it. It's that All Presence, that God, permeating every aspect of my life which I think is a healthy sort of Christianity. It's something which we sometimes get away from when we stick God up in heaven or we stick him in a church. I'm not saying he isn't in heaven or in a church, but I'm just saying that God is within the human being, you don't have to go searching for him.

From Psalm 139

O Lord, you search me and you know me!
You know my resting and my rising;
You discern my purpose from afar.
You mark when I walk or lie down,
All my ways lie open to you.

Before ever a word is on my tongue,
You know it, O Lord, through and through.
Behind and before you besiege me,
Your hand ever laid upon me.
Too wonderful for me this knowledge;
Too high beyond my reach.

For it was you who created my being,
Knit me together in my mother's womb.
I thank you for the wonders of my being.
For the wonders of all your creation!
To me how mysterious your thoughts,
The sum of them not to be numbered.
If I count them they are more than the sand.
To finish, I must be eternal like you.

O search me, God, and know my heart!
O test me and know my thoughts!
See that I follow not the wrong path,
And lead me to the path of life eternal.

●

THE MOST REVEREND GEORGE NOAKES,
Archbishop of Wales

On his chosen Easter prayer

It's a prayer that's based on Christ's appearance to disciples on
the road to Emmaus. I think that the road to Emmaus is the
road that leads home from the graveyard, as it were. It's a road
that all of us have had to travel at some time in our life. It's the
road of disillusionment, bitterness, despair. You can hear in
the voices of these two disciples as they travel along the road,
'We had hoped,' they say, and how often you and I have said
that – hopes dashed, dreams shattered. Now that's the road to
Emmaus, the road that leads from the Cross.

The disciples didn't recognise Christ when he walked with
them, and this is again so true of my experience of life. This
Christ of ours, he's always been the unexpected Christ: he
wasn't expected to be born in a stable in Bethlehem, Judea; and
he wasn't expected on the storm-tossed sea of Galilee; and
certainly he wasn't expected to be seen alive on the third day

after his crucifixion. This has been my experience in life. Very often when I least expect him, there he is. I should imagine that this is one of the great discoveries, to know that this risen Christ is walking with you. That's the joy of Easter to me.

Can I use a story?

I remember hearing about an atheist who had a little boy and the atheist was determined that this little boy wasn't going to hear anything about God. He came home for tea one day and the first question the little boy asked him was, 'Who is God?' Now this man was something of a psychologist and all he did was to put a little cardboard strip on the boy's bedroom wall. The strip said, 'God is nowhere'. This strip was the last thing the little boy saw before he went to bed at night and the first thing he saw in the morning.

After three days the father went into the little boy's bedroom. He saw that the little boy had drawn a line between the 'W' and the 'H'. 'God is nowhere' had become 'God is now here'.

I think this is the joy of the resurrection. When I feel sometimes, as we all feel, that we've lost him and that he isn't there; when we shout out in agony of mind and spirit, 'Where is God?' then here he is. That is the discovery of Easter for me.

My faith is very simple. I find no difficulty with the resurrection at all. Because I believe that Jesus is the Son of God I don't see anything wrong in having a miraculous beginning, if you like, and a miraculous ending. I am very happy to accept this. Also my experience of life has been of the presence, the abiding presence of this Christ. When you know that, you're not too concerned about the academic exercise.

Compiled by the Most Reverend George Noakes, from various prayers

O Living Lord, who on the first Easter Day didst reveal thyself to thy disciples as the conqueror of sin and death, go with us on our journey through this world. Guide us, uphold us, strengthen us, make our hearts to burn within us and evermore manifest thyself to our souls in gracious and heavenly power. We ask this for thine own name's sake.   Amen.

•

DR KATHLEEN RAINE, poet, critic, and writer on William Blake

On her chosen meditation

When I ask myself what my greatest problem with myself is, I come to the theme – forgiveness. I find forgiveness very difficult to understand. Blake seemed to understand forgiveness better than any other Christian writer known to me. In fact he made it absolutely central to the Christian religion. He saw forgiveness as the uniquely Christian virtue. He said that all the pagan virtues had been defined by Plato and Socrates but only Jesus taught forgiveness.

As one grows older, one becomes more and more aware of the long, long record of things that we've done wrong, mistakes we've made. Sometimes this realisation becomes almost unbearable, and if we take the view of ourselves, 'I am what I have done,' there seems to be no room for forgiveness in that. We are simply the sum of our sins and by the end of our life we're simply a write-off. Now that's the end of all possible hope. When we're young we can hope to do better, we can still hope to be good; but at the end of a life we have to look instead at our accumulated sins, mistakes, call it what you like.

Blake's understanding was like this. He said that we should 'distinguish between the man and his present state'. What he meant was that because there is in each of us a portion of the eternal divine light, the Divine Being – 'Jesus the Imagination' were Blake's words, 'Jesus himself' – because of that, we are not simply the sum of what we have done. Because that eternal spark, light, is always itself, therefore we can always find in that 'divine humanity', as Blake said, 'the divine presence', so there is room to change and to be something other than the sum of what we have done. That is forgiveness.

That eternal presence, that divine humanity, call it the God within, is always present in everyone and therefore it is not only possible for us to forgive other people because that is in them; but it's also possible for us to forgive ourselves which I think many of us find to be a great deal more difficult than to forgive other people. To forgive ourselves, that's the ultimate forgiveness.

Meditation from *The Everlasting Gospel*
William Blake (1757–1827)

There is not one moral virtue that Jesus Inculcated but Plato and Cicero did Inculcate before him: what then did Christ inculcate? Forgiveness of sins. This alone is the gospel and this is the Life and Immortality brought to light by Jesus, Even the Covenant of Jehovah which is This: If you forgive one another your trespasses, so shall Jehovah forgive you, that he himself may dwell among you.

Mutual forgiveness of each vice
These are the Gates of Paradise

●

**DAVID HOBMAN, television presenter, formerly
Director of Age Concern**

On his chosen prayer

I might have doubts about my theology, but I'm absolutely certain about the moment in the worship service which for me is very moving. It's when we say, 'Peace be with you,' to each other. For me it epitomises the religious impulse because it's really about the body and the mind and the soul. We put out our hands to each other, and that's very important, because touching people is very significant – the love of bodies, of persons. Then it moves to another plane, because it's also about the mind and about the soul.

If I wish you peace, in a political sense I wish you to live in a world which is peaceful and a world which is just, a world which is decent. Finally and ultimately, I wish you peace within yourself. I suppose this inner personal peace is about the spirit. I really don't believe we can have peace in the world if we don't have peace within ourselves and I don't think we can live in peace in isolation. We're not all born to be hermits; we have to live within the community and if we live within the community we have to touch the community.

As I grow older I find it both easier and more difficult to find peace within myself. The passing of time and the loss of time create human urgency; there are more things to be done and less time in which to do them. Yet in another sense, the fierce

13

drive, the ambitions which I had as a younger man, ambitions to achieve things and to change the world and advance myself, these diminish. I'm less disturbed about the mistakes I've made in the past and the things I've done which I shouldn't have done. I have to admit, though, that I also get more impatient at times than I used to. One changes in so many ways, but I think it's easier to find quietness and peace within myself now than it was when I was younger.

My understanding of being a neighbour, of neighbourliness, came to me from my parents. My father taught me to understand how to be intolerant about evil but to be enormously tolerant of people who behaved in a stupid, strange or uncaring way. I think one has to separate these two. I suppose from my mother, who was very passionate and very interested in the way that people lived, there's a need within myself to understand and to come to terms with the people who are around me.

Peace follows great joy, as peace may follow great sadness. I'm not too sure if peace is part of the exultant feeling of joy, but it's certainly about calmness, and it's certainly about serenity. It's about the capacity to step a little aside from overwhelming worries, worries which change us from being rational, enjoyable human beings to becoming somewhat paranoid.

Prayer from the liturgy of the Christian Church

Peace be with you.

●

ELIZABETH LONGFORD, writer

On her chosen prayer

The prayer speaks about eventide, and this can be taken as eventide in two senses. It's a prayer which we can use as the shadows of the day lengthen at evening, and we can use it when we're coming to the evening of our lives, or at any rate the late afternoon.

The words speak of God being our support and I can't imagine life without feeling that God is here with me. I'm not aware of this all the time, because, as this prayer mentions, the fevers and business of the world do distract me. But even so, these moments of distraction don't destroy my feeling of God being very present with me. I just can't imagine a life without that feeling. What would be there? You can't imagine a blank – a blank is a nothing and we can't imagine a nothing.

Looking into the future I have two sets of feelings. One set is bound absolutely, inextricably and closely with people I love here. I can't think of leaving them as being anything but a sorrow. But, in the other way, I feel we're united together through the fact that we're all immortal. I don't feel we finish when we finish, and so in a sense I look forward to what's going to happen, though of course none of us can imagine what life after death will be like. I don't believe in golden bells or pearly gates, though I love singing about them. I think it's a beautiful metaphor.

The after-life doesn't really worry me. I suppose if my life got slower and slower I'd try and focus my imagination more on the future and on what immortality can possibly mean, but I have glimpses of it now.

Occasionally, say out on a walk, or out in the garden, at a moment of great beauty and great peace, I suddenly have a kind of mystical feeling of unity with something much bigger and more serene than myself. At such times I imagine that the after-life may be a state of being with God in that sense, that wonderful sense of unity with the whole. In this life there are moments when one feels cut off from something one ought to be joined on to and so the after-life must be exactly the opposite to that. One must feel joined on to something that one has been cut off from.

Prayer by John Henry Newman (1801–90)

May he support us all the day long, till the shades lengthen, and the evening comes, and the busy world is hushed, and the fever of life is over, and our work is done. Then in his mercy may he give us a safe lodging, and a holy rest, and peace at the last.

•

AIR CHIEF MARSHAL SIR ALASDAIR STEEDMAN,
Controller of the Royal Air Force Benevolent Fund

On his chosen prayer

My love of this prayer goes back a very long time. I had a marvellous English teacher at school who instilled into me a great love of language and this prayer was one of his favourites.

Then later on in life the prayer came back to me again and again. I was twice lent to overseas governments during my service with the Royal Air Force – once to Ceylon, now Sri Lanka; and once to Malaysia – and I found the prayer of extraordinary use to demonstrate the need to be persistent. Anybody can start things; it really is the following them through that's important.

I say the prayer to myself a lot. It's also a prayer that tends to be heard quite a lot at Thanksgiving services and it's an occupational hazard of the Controller of the Royal Air Force Benevolent Fund to attend such services. I always love it.

The prayer refers to 'the true virtue'. I think the true virtue is to see what is good and to do it despite difficulties.

On prayer

Prayer is immensely important to me. It's a comfort to me, and it's a particular comfort now that I'm a widower. All my life, because I was brought up in the Christian tradition, I've had recourse to prayer. I don't think I would have been strong enough to meet the challenges in my life if I hadn't had prayer to fall back on. My faith is a very deep rooted one. I hope it's not too overt, but it's immensely comforting to me.

My prayer life is absolutely spontaneous. I suppose the first time I really started praying spontaneously was when I was terribly frightened during the war, as I was quite often.

I think you can only fall back on your faith if you've had it rooted in you from early childhood, but certainly when you're in conditions which can be appalling, and certainly terribly frightening, it's a comfort to be able to communicate in the way that you can with prayer. Although I suppose it's wrong in principle only to be asking for things when you're suddenly in need, there's no denying that it makes life a great deal easier for you at the time. I'm not talking about flying operations, because when you're actually flying and involved in things you don't have time to be frightened. It's in retrospect, or it's when you're in the cold light of dawn before you go up, that you tend to feel the need for prayer. At least that was the case with me.

Prayer attributed to Sir Francis Drake (c. 1540–96)

O Lord God, when thou givest to thy servants to endeavour any great matter, grant us also to know that it is not the beginning, but the continuing of the same unto the end until it be thoroughly finished, which yieldeth the true virtue. Through him who for the finishing of thy work laid down his life, Jesus Christ our Lord.   Amen.

●

REVEREND MOELWYN MERCHANT, poet, sculptor, theologian, former canon at Salisbury Cathedral and Professor of English at Exeter University

On his chosen meditation

'What doth the Lord require of thee, but to do justly, to love mercy and to walk humbly with thy God.' It seems to me that in those three words – 'justly', 'mercy' and 'humbly' – you have the height of the Jewish understanding of the relationship of man to man and of man to God.

I think we have to go back to the Hebrew understanding of what those abstractions really mean. 'To do justly.' It doesn't say to do justice. It is to *behave* justly with your fellow man and through behaving justly you may get some conception of what justice is. But it doesn't matter if you don't. It isn't prescriptions from outside that tell you, you must do this or that; it isn't even the ten commandments; it is through following your own inner voice, your inner conscience and your knowledge of what God requires, that you do justly.

The verbs are also very special. It's an absolute demand. It isn't, 'What then does God gently ask you to do, that he would like you to do, and that perhaps if you, out of the goodness of your heart, would do it, he would be very pleased.' No. It is, 'What does the Lord *require* of thee.' It's a demand.

Then you move from 'justly' to 'love mercy'. The Hebrew

word that we've translated as 'mercy', combines loving-kindness, compassion, sympathy, the imaginative understanding of one heart by another. It means that in loving kindness we really do relate one to the other.

But the third command I find to be the richest of all, and in some ways the most fearful. We have somehow or other, in awe, in questfulness, in the attempt really to understand what we are as human beings and what God is as Deity, to walk very delicately. So Micah says, 'and walk humbly with God'. There is no other way. There's no security, there's no sureness by which we can know God. We simply somehow say that there is a great being on whom we are wholly dependent, and knowing our dependence as children, we walk humbly. The word 'humbly', is the enhancement of everything that we know as love. The kind of humility that someone in love has for the loved person; walking humbly because there is something so delicate there, more delicate than a butterfly, more delicate than a flower; and it's something that we dare not presume upon, we dare not crush.

From the Book of Micah

What doth the Lord require of thee, but
to do justly,
to love mercy and
to walk humbly with thy God.

●

WENDY CRAIG, actress

On her chosen prayer

The prayer speaks of us as being God's treasures, and I think the idea of us being God's treasures is terribly important because far too often we denigrate ourselves, we put ourselves down and feel unworthy. Being God's treasures means that we mustn't think in those ways, if he treasures us then we must be of worth.

I really lacked confidence. I found it very difficult to go into a room where there were a lot of people. I also suffered a lot from guilty feelings. Since I've become a Christian I don't have those feelings any more because now I know that I just take

18

those feelings to Jesus and say, 'This is how I am, I'm sorry for the things that are making me feel guilty,' and I know that he'll forgive me because he promised in his word that he would. I ask him to help me not to do these things again and immediately I feel at peace and strong and restored. This is a wonderful feeling because I can walk around, not proudly, but not cringing and not so humble that I can't look anyone in the eyes – not that I was ever as bad as that, but it can get almost that bad at times.

You see I think I had a feeling that life was pointless. I couldn't understand why I was here or what we were all doing here, it all seemed pretty pointless. Sure, I had the love of my family and I had my work and all the good things, but there was some deep, deep motivation missing inside me. If you feel that life is pointless it becomes worthless and this is why I often felt worthless. This must happen to a lot of people, but it doesn't need to. It's what you are that matters; it's what's going on inside that matters and if you're sure that God truly loves you and treasures you, then you can go through all kinds of circumstances feeling confident. Confident and full of worth, indeed, one of God's treasured children.

The prayer also affects how I feel and look at other people. It makes me realise that everyone is very important to God. He has no favourites.

Prayer by John Donne (1573–1631)

Eternal and most glorious God, who has stamped the soul of man with thine image, received it into thy revenue and made it a part of thy treasure; suffer us not so to undervalue ourselves, nay, so to impoverish thee, as to give away these souls for nothing, and all the world is nothing, if the soul must be given for it. Do this, O God, for his sake who knows our natural infirmities, for he had them and knows the weight of our sins for he paid a dear price for them, thy son, our Saviour, Jesus Christ. Amen.

●

JOHN CASSON, theatrical director and management consultant in communication

The story behind his meditation

During the 1940s I was a prisoner of war in Germany. . . . I'd always been interested in philosophical and religious questions and so I spent my first year reading theology in such books as were available. There were a lot of things that puzzled me and I thought the experts in the field would be able to answer them for me. But the more I went on reading, the more I found the experts didn't answer the questions for me. So I took a decision, a conscious decision. I said, 'I'm going to start absolutely all over again. I'm going to say that I don't believe in anything and I'm going to see what happens. I'm going to start from scratch.' And this is what I did.

For a month there was a sort of emptiness, then suddenly things that had appeared paradoxical before started to fall into place. I found that instead of talking about good and evil and so on, I said, instead, either one is harmonious or one is discordant. This way of thinking was probably brought to my mind because in the prison camp we had been doing a production of *The Messiah*, and I was singing heavy bass. Then one day I discovered that as long as I was listening to the music of the whole and knew my part and didn't have to think about it; as long as I was in harmony with the choir, I had the extraordinary sensation that I wasn't one tiny lost individual, but my personality had expanded to take in the whole. I had, as it were, become the choir, temporarily.

Well, it seems to me that praying is trying to do that on a vast scale and most of us are not going to achieve it, certainly not in our lifetimes, . . . but I rather go with Joyce Grenfell who once said that when she prayed she wasn't petitioning, she wasn't asking for anything for herself, instead she was trying by praying to align herself with whatever it is that is meaningful in the universe.

The lines I wrote, based on my experiences in Germany, touch on time and eternity. I don't like the idea of eternity being our time going on and on and on. I like to think of eternity as one gigantic now. Everything is now to the Almighty in some extraordinary way. The lines also help me in my dealings with other people. They help to get me away from judging them. You remember Christ said, 'Judge not, that ye be not judged.' Well, I constantly tell myself that it isn't a question of saying that I judge someone, but rather of asking myself why that person thinks that whatever they're doing is right; why they can't see that what they're doing is discordant; why sometimes *I* can't see that what I'm doing is discordant. This harmony is at least a standard that one can work back to.

On God

I think my response to God is one both of awe and reassurance. Reassurance because I am part of this immensity, but awe because one is very humble, one is very small compared with the vastness of God. But it is most reassuring to know that in some extraordinary way one is part of the Almighty, one is a microscopic little limb stretching out from the Almighty.

Lines written by John Casson

I am the cosmic vastness,
Perfected and never begun.
Eternal and instantaneous,
Multi-dimensional,
One.

•

THE RIGHT REVEREND MARK SANTER, Bishop of Birmingham

On his choice of prayer

This prayer reflects many of the concerns of St Augustine of Hippo (354–430), the famous phrase in his *Confessions* when he asks God to help us to love what God commands and to give us that which he has promised. There's also Augustine's sense that human beings are, you might almost call it, a zoo of desires and affections and that the grace of God works on us in the years of our pilgrimage on earth to order and rightly direct our loves and affections. Augustine makes it clear again and again that it isn't that people have to be told to love. Everyone loves something. The problem is what we love and how strongly we love it.

We live in a very turbulent and disordered time and we feel

that turbulence and disorder within ourselves because we pick up much of the goings-on around us. Augustine lived at a time when the Roman Empire was beginning to fall to pieces around him and he had a deep sense of the contrast between the transience and changeability of this world – a world which was good because God had made it, but a world still transient in nature – and the eternal, unchanging goodness of God which is what we have to love.

Love is absolutely basic. In talking so much about love Augustine was picking up the commandments in the Gospel, 'Thou shalt love the Lord thy God with all thy heart and with all thy soul and with all thy mind and with all thy strength and thou shalt love thy neighbour as thyself.' Augustine was concerned that people loved things that were not ultimate as if they were ultimate and this turned the objects of their love into idols. It seems to me to be something that's very important to this present time when people have so much lost or missed their sense of the transcendence and Being of God, and have instead set their affections and their hope of immortality on things that are essentially transient, things like possessions; possession of power over other people as well as possessions of goods and money.

The prayer also asks for obedience. It's not easy to be obedient. As I look back each day on how the day has gone, I realise ways in which I have let myself be distracted from the things to which I should have been giving primary attention. The important thing then, is not so much to say, 'I will be obedient,' but rather to put myself in the hands of God and ask for the grace to be obedient.

On daily prayer

I've discovered I simply can't live without prayer. I'm extremely fortunate here in that I have a colleague, a chaplain who lives next door, who prays with me mornings and evenings. The fact that we can do this together as well as the time I have to pray on my own is, in a sense, the centre round which the rest of my life circles.

Prayer for the Fourth Sunday after Easter,
Book of Common Prayer

O Almighty God, who alone canst order the unruly wills and

affections of sinful men: Grant unto thy people, that they may love the thing which thou commandest, and desire that which thou dost promise; That so, among the sundry and manifold changes of the world, our hearts may surely there be fixed, where true joys are to be found; through Jesus Christ our Lord. Amen.

●

THE REVEREND ANN GURNEY, former head deaconess in the Diocese of London

On her chosen prayer

It is a very brief prayer and, for me at any rate, a prayer full of meaning.

It's a prayer which was written in a book which was really, I suppose, the private spiritual diary of Dag Hammarskjöld, one time secretary-general of the United Nations. The prayer comes from the book *Markings*. It is a prayer of just two lines:

> For all that has been, thanks.
> For all that shall be, yes.

I think the word 'yes' is something which I use as a sort of repetitive prayer. When I use it I have a great deal in mind that anyone hearing me would not understand.

I use the prayer also sometimes for commitment. I think it really is a prayer of faith. When one looks back over one's life, quite often one thinks that there are things in life for which one doesn't want to give thanks. This prayer says to me that I have to look at my life and say: yes, there have been failures on my part; yes, there have been disappointments, there have been bereavements and such things which at the time seemed terrible. But, with the perspective of years, one can see how God used those situations and how our lives have developed since then in a different way. This different way may have been the way that God wanted.

As far as my own failures go, they're significant and they're important, but I would still say that God's acceptance of me and his forgiveness of me are far more important.

Because I can give thanks for the past, I feel I can commit myself to the future. 'Yes' is a very affirmative word. For me it

23

means saying yes to life, not the kind of life that I had fantasies about in my youth, but the life that I now know is mine. It means saying yes to people, not just the people who I particularly feel drawn towards, but people whom I meet generally. It means being open to whatever life has to offer me – being open in the strong faith, I hope, that God will be with me and see me through. Therefore I can commit myself in the fullest sort of way.

I believe too that it's a matter of saying yes to myself, to those aspects of myself which I would prefer not to be there – my shadow side – but aspects which are very important parts of my being.

**From *Markings*
*Dag Hammarskjöld (1905–61)***

For all that has been, thanks.
To all that shall be, yes.

•

THE ARCHBISHOP OF CANTERBURY, THE MOST REVEREND AND RIGHT HONOURABLE DR ROBERT RUNCIE

*On St Stephen**

He died at the hands of a howling mob without fear, looking to the Lord Jesus and praying, as Jesus did, for his enemies. All through the centuries there have been dramatic and undramatic examples of those who showed that trust in time of trial. Indeed, we shouldn't be remembering the birth of Christ 2000 years after the event unless there had been those who witnessed to the power of that love which comes through Christmas.

On fear

I think that fear is very central to human experience and I think that it's very much dealt with in the Christian faith because Jesus never contrasts belief with unbelief, but rather contrasts it with fear. He sometimes says, 'Why are you so fearful, have you no faith,' and when St John wants to sum up the effect of the coming of our Lord into the world he says that perfect love casts out not evil, not sin, but fear. I think that if we were absolutely honest in our private moments, and sometimes these are quite painful moments, we find that we're often dogged by fear of others – what they will think, fear of failure and the consequences of it, fear of illness or inadequacy, fear of death. Socially fear sometimes wrecks marriages, through fear friendships are thrown over, communities broken up. Then there are all those irrational fears, fears over which we have no control.

Now God doesn't wave a magic wand and protect us from the things that happen to other people. He enables us to meet them without fear whenever we know ourselves to be totally loved. That's the message of Christmas, I believe. That could be a cosy message, but today, on St Stephen's Day, the cosiness undoubtedly gives place to courage.

I wouldn't want you to think that I'm a person who doesn't fear and doesn't have great anxieties, but I know that the whole wonder of the Christian faith is that when we open ourselves to God coming towards us, and when we really allow him to work within us, then there's the beginning, and then there's also the growth in that sort of courage which comes from being loved.

It's fear and selfishness which undermine well-being in life and it is the love of God for us and our generosity in return for that love which constitute the antidote to fear and self-centredness.

Prayer of St Theresa of Avila (1515–82)

Let nothing disturb thee
Nothing affright thee
All things are passing
God never changeth
Patient endurance
Attaineth to all things
Who God possesseth
In nothing is wanting
Alone God sufficeth.

* This conversation was broadcast on St Stephen's Day, 1987. Dr Runcie often begins the day with this prayer, which is referred to as St Theresa's 'Bookmark'. When he was ordained priest, Dr Runcie was given a prayer book which had this prayer pasted in it.

ANTON PHILLIPS, founder and Director of Carib Theatre Productions

On the meditation of his choice

We recently put on a production of Kahlil Gibran's *The Prophet*, and listening to it, night after night, I came to like the book even more than I had done before. Certain passages in it appealed directly to me; the truths in them hit me in no uncertain manner.

The Prophet is asked a question: 'Tell us about Religion?' And he speaks about religion in a passage which comes back to me over and over. The thought that he conveys is that everything we do is an act of religion. We can't separate our daily lives from any sort of religious belief that we have; we have to see all our actions and all our thoughts as acts which are right or wrong. The passage embodies the fact that we should lead the good life, and not just live this good life on a Sunday.

I can't say that I'm constantly aware of the spiritual dimension in my daily life but that old biblical phrase 'Do unto others', that's a concept that I certainly try to live by. I try to behave in a way which is correct by my moral standards, which aren't necessarily those reflecting a specific Christian ethic. I guess what I try to do is to behave in a way which is not likely to do harm to anyone, a way which hopefully will uplift my life and the lives of those people around me. As I'm involved in theatre I try to make my work as uplifting and exciting as possible. People ought to come out of the theatre feeling better than when they went in, they should feel moved in an up-beat way by what they've seen, and moved to behave in a better way towards themselves and towards others.

The passage speaks of 'the house of my soul'. I'm not sure that I completely recognise my soul as such in my life. In a way everyone has to determine for himself what the house of his soul is. For me it's a more all-embracing definition. The soul and the body and the mind, our behaviour and the work that we do, the way we're entertained, all of that makes up a composite, if you wish, of the house of the soul. In all of that I try, not always successfully, to keep those windows of my soul open from 'dawn to dawn'.

From *The Prophet*
Kahlil Gibran (1883–1931)

Who can separate his faith from his actions, or his belief from
his occupations?

Who can spread his hours before him, saying, 'This for God
and this for myself; this for my soul and this for my body'?

All your hours are wings that beat through space from self to
self.

He who wears his morality but as his best garment were better
naked; . . .

And he to whom worshipping is a window, to open but also to
shut, has not yet visited the house of his soul whose
windows are from dawn to dawn.

•

DON ROSE, Personnel Director at Woolworths

On his chosen prayer

I find that after something like thirty odd years in commercial
life, there's a certain arrogance creeps in to the way you
conduct your affairs. I think I needed to be reminded that I
might have been this way before; I might have dealt with the
same questions and the same problems, but there's not always
the same answer. I also wanted to show that in dealing with
people at varying stages in their business experience I should be
able to listen to them first, and then with a reasonable sense of
humility talk to them about a solution to whatever problems
they had brought to me. So I began to look for something
which would give me a vision for this relationship and I
remembered this seventeenth-century nun's prayer. When I
re-read it, I found there something like fourteen or fifteen
precepts which really would safeguard me from becoming just
a crusty old man.

Essentially it's a plea on the part of the supplicant to be saved
from becoming the sort of person who thinks that there's
nothing else to be learnt, that there's very little life is bringing
you which is new. If you become like that, you get the sort of
arrogance and cocksuredness which can spoil relationships.

The other thing is that we're prone to see the worst side of people and the latter part of the prayer is a supplication to see good in everyone. This seems to me to be a good motto for relationships.

There's a part of the prayer that talks about memory. I'm finding now that at this awful age of fifty-three, I can't remember things as easily as I used to. My colleagues and friends sometimes laugh at me when I say, 'Oh dear, I should have remembered that.' There's a lovely part in the prayer which says, 'Look, I know my memory isn't improving, but guard me against over-aggressiveness in trying to cover up my lapses of memory.'

Seventeenth-century nun's prayer

Lord thou knowest better than I know myself that I am growing older and will some day be old. Keep me from the fatal habit of thinking I must say something on every subject and on every occasion.

Release me from craving to straighten out everybody's affairs. Make me thoughtful but not moody; helpful but not bossy. With my vast store of wisdom it seems a pity not to use it all, but thou knowest, Lord, that I want a few friends at the end.

Keep my mind free from the recital of endless details; give me wings to get to the point. Seal my lips on my aches and pains. They are increasing and the love of rehearsing them is becoming sweeter as the years go by. I dare not ask for grace enough to enjoy the tales of others' pains, but help me to endure them with patience.

I dare not ask for improved memory, but for a growing humility and a lessening cocksureness when my memory seems to clash with the memories of others. Teach me the glorious lesson that occasionally I may be mistaken.

Keep me reasonably sweet; I do not want to be a saint – some of them are so hard to live with – but a sour old person is one of the crowning works of the devil. Give me the ability to see good things in unexpected places and talents in unexpected people. And give me, O Lord, the grace to tell them so. Amen.

THE REVEREND SHEILA WATSON, Deacon of the Church of England

On her chosen prayer

It's one of the few prayers which immediately I heard I wanted to memorise because I somehow wanted it to be part of myself, to be something that I carried around with me.

I think one of the difficulties that there can be with prayer is – where do we begin. There are times when we're feeling lost, when we're just overwhelmed by something that might be a personal tragedy, that might be a situation where we just don't know what to do, or that might be hearing of some terrible suffering or pain of other people . . . and this prayer which begins, 'Lord, I know not what to ask of thee,' gives me something that's in tune with that feeling of being lost and not knowing where to start.

The prayer gives us a reassurance of God's love and God's care and God's understanding of our needs. It's not that the prayer is going to change how we feel, but it reminds us of a faith which says that God is love and that in that love God shares our pain. To me that's what the story of Jesus and the Cross is all about.

So often we fall into the trap of attending to our superficial needs or to the needs of our own or other people that are squealing the loudest, rather than to our real, deepest needs. There's an obvious example of that in someone like an addict who craves for something which may actually destroy him or her and that's not their real need. But I don't see that as a trap only for addicts; it's something which we all fall into only too easily. I see this prayer very much as a reminder of that, of asking us actually to take the time to begin to look at our real needs and to work with God on that.

From a prayer of Metropolitan Philaret of Moscow (1553–1633)

O Lord, I know not what to ask of thee.
Thou alone knowest what are my true needs.
Thou lovest me more than I myself know how to love.
Help me to see my real needs that are concealed from me;
Through Jesus Christ our Lord.   Amen.

FATHER MICHAEL FORTUNATO, Russian Orthodox priest at the Cathedral of the Dormition and All Saints, London

On the Holy Spirit

The Holy Spirit is a person. He is a wise and comforting presence, a gift of God to man, perhaps the greatest gift ever. Has he been neglected? I think he has in many ways.

It's very important to realise that we in the West have become very indifferent to the bond which exists between the spirit and matter, between the material element and the spiritual element. Various people have gone either towards materialism or towards spiritualism. It's very difficult to find where the balance is. I would say that the difference is not between matter and spirit because both were created by God. The difference is between the created life and the Creator himself, the Spirit. In that sense the Holy Spirit is the omnipotent creator, the one who has made everything, the one to whom we should turn. He is among us to remind us that we are all his children.

To understand the Spirit is the task of a lifetime; it's growing into the understanding of God. I think one can understand the coming of Christ as preparatory to the coming of the Spirit. There is a text in our liturgy which says that Pentecost, when the Spirit came to man, is the greatest of the Feasts, the ultimate Feast, because God came to dwell with us for good, for ever. In fact that's what the Kingdom of God is. In Christ God became man, then he went to his father for a time – and we live in that time – and in his place he sent the Comforter, the Holy Spirit at Pentecost.

Christ is vivid. Everybody knows his story – it's part of our literature, part of our culture – but the Holy Spirit is almost our future as well as being the present. He is the token of a future in which God and man will live together, sharing everything. He is vitality. He is dynamic. His energy is perhaps that face of God which is turned towards the world, the face that makes us able to reach up to heaven and to his life.

Prayer from the Russian Orthodox Pentecost liturgy

O Heavenly King,
O Comforter,

The Spirit of Truth
Who art in all places
And fillest all things;
The treasure of blessings
And giver of life;
Come and abide in us,
Cleanse us from all impurity,
And in thy goodness
Save our souls.

•

DR SWEE CHAI ANG, surgeon and founder of Medical Aid for Palestinians, the non-political charity which sends out medical staff to the Palestinian refugee camps in the Middle East

On her Christian faith

Initially when I was trapped in the middle of the massacre at Sabra and Shatila refugee camps I felt that God had left us. Now I understand that he has not left us. I went to Israel after the massacres to address the Commission of Inquiry which was set up there into the events. I went to Bethlehem and as I was standing before the birthplace of Christ, I knew that for many, many years man had sinned and betrayed God. God has not left us but we have sinned against him.

On prayer

I think prayer is the only thing that has kept me spiritually alive, that has kept my faith in God. When I find myself in a desperate situation, when people are dying around me, when I feel that I may be killed at any moment, I tell God, 'My life is in your hands, and if this is the moment for me to die, then give me the strength that I need.' Prayer is the only key. Of course, most of us try to work a lot, we're always busy, but we have to remember to pray.

When I'm away from the Lebanon and here in London making preparations to return there I find that I pray even more than when I'm there. Here it's autumn now, and autumn is usually one of my favourite seasons because it's when I start looking forward to Christmas, but this year I can't have a happy Christmas. I know that there are thousands and thousands of people who are homeless in Lebanon as a result of the attacks on the refugee camps; the children have no roof over their heads and the women are suffering because they watch their children suffer and when the rain starts to pour they will die. It's a human tragedy and it will be a miracle if the camps can be reconstructed in time, but I believe in miracles and I believe in God.

Prayer by Dr Swee Chai Ang

Lord Jesus, thank you for the morning. Let us open our eyes and see your beauty. Today we might have bad times; there might be things that try us, some of us might have no money to pay the rent, we might have no money to heat our rooms or we might be worried about our jobs, children might be sick, but Lord, we know that you understand.

So Father, this day when we wake up to all the troubles of the world and when we open a newspaper and we see all the areas of disasters, all the fighting, we remember the love of the Lord.

May that love stay in our hearts always and give us strength to bear whatever burden we have to bear. Not that we deserve all these qualities, but because you in your kindness have offered it.

Give us the humility to accept your gift and the intelligence to treasure it always. In Jesus' name, we ask this.   Amen.

•

THE VERY REVEREND HUGH MONTEFIORE, Lord Bishop of Birmingham, 1983–87, and during those years a very outspoken member of the Church of England and House of Lords, and Chairman of the Church of England's Board for Social Responsibility

On living

The only way I cope with life at all is to try to live in the present. If I look back to the past, then I get filled with guilt and all sorts of things like that; but if I look to the future then I'm really talking about the unknown and it's no good living in cloud cuckoo land, so quite honestly next week's the unknown and when it comes it comes.*

I've had to develop this outlook, develop it living under stress for the most part. When I was at the university church Great St Mary's in Cambridge I used to have a great notice up on the office board, 'NOTHING REALLY MATTERS' – not 'nothing matters', but 'nothing *really* matters' – and I think I had to teach myself this habit of living for each day, one day at a time, during that period. You have to do this otherwise you get consumed by worry; you don't live.

I think to do this you have to have things that engross your attention, things that fascinate you and make you concentrate. When you don't have such things in your life then it becomes very difficult indeed.

You know one has to have both quietness and activity in life, one without the other means that there's something very unbalanced. At the moment I have a period of quiet at the beginning of the day which I spend in chapel. Without this quiet time I don't think I could cope with the business of the day.

On retirement

I think it's a rather good preparation for the life to come. First of all I've got to learn to be, rather than to do, because you don't do so much in retirement. Secondly I think it's right there should be a pause if possible in life, when you think of the eternal things which after all await us all. So I look on it as a sort of preparation for death, though I hope that death won't come for a long time. . . . Yes, there's always fear. I often say my retirement is rather like dying . . . you're full of faith that this is the gateway to life but you'd actually rather like to know just what it's like on the other side.

On his chosen prayer

I've always been rather moved by this prayer and at the present time it really hits me. You see, it speaks of acceptance, and acceptance is the thing which people find most difficult in life and which we need God's grace to help us with. Then, when we're changing our lifestyle we need courage. . . . At the moment I also feel that I need wisdom in good judgement to know the things I should do and the things I shouldn't do.

These are the three points of the prayer which hit me most at the moment.

Prayer by Reinhold Niebuhr (1892–1971)

Give us, Lord,
The courage to change those things that can be changed,
The patience to bear those things that cannot be changed,
And the wisdom to know the difference,
Through Jesus Christ our Lord.   Amen.

* I spoke with Bishop Montefiore a few days before his retirement.

•

WENDY TYNDALE, Head of the Latin American and Caribbean group, Christian Aid

On her chosen prayer

The way the prayer begins, 'Our Father, who is in us here on earth', is a great challenge to us. The poor in Latin America certainly don't conceive of God as a divine intervener in their lives. They see that God only acts through them. The theme of the prayer is building up the kingdom beginning here on earth, and the only way God can act is through us.

The prayer also challenges us because the poor in Central America don't see Christianity as only concerned with individuals. They, like the prophets in the Old Testament, have a very strong sense of a God of justice who is on their side in their struggle to get what they need to live on – land, fair wages. What they are saying to us is very understandable in our terms here. We must think of justice here in terms of us buying very cheap coffee in supermarkets when those who have planted and picked the coffee are struggling for their very existence.

The prayer says 'forgive us for keeping silent in the face of injustice and for burying our dreams'. I think here we're talking about burying idealism, that we come to accept injustices as they are and think we can do nothing about them so we just don't notice them. This is the opposite of keeping idealism alive.

Only through our links with the people with whom we work am I able to keep my dreams alive. Their message comes through very strongly in this prayer. It's a prayer full of hope and of trust – of trust in God and of trust in human kind and in life.

The people who wrote this in El Salvador know that if they carry on struggling, 'being a cool breeze for those who sweat', as they put it, that in the end God's kingdom will at least have begun to have been built here on earth.

From a version of the Lord's Prayer used in villages in El Salvador

Our Father,
who is in us here on earth

Holy is your name
in the hungry who share their bread and their song.

Your kingdom come,
a generous land where confidence and truth reign.

Let us do your will,
being a cool breeze for those who sweat.

You are giving us our daily bread
when we manage to get back our lands
or to get a fairer wage.

Forgive us
for keeping silent in the face of injustice
and for burying our dreams.

Don't let us fall into the temptation
of taking up the same arms as the enemy,

But deliver us from evil which disunites us
and we shall have believed in humanity and in life
and we shall have known your kingdom
which is being built for ever and ever.

•

FATHER BILL KIRKPATRICK, co-founder of
Reaching-Out, a listening and counselling service, and a
priest associate of the Sisters of the Love of God, a
contemplative community based in Oxford. Father Bill is
in the ninth year of his Listening Ministry in Earls Court
where his door stays open for all who would like to share
their burden with him.

On prayer in his daily life

Prayer is my time to be with myself so that I can be with the
mystery we call God. In being with these two mysteries,
myself and God, I can perhaps be totally with myself with
another person and look into the mystery of that person who is
searching. So for me prayer is crucial. Prayer is being in the
activity of listening and more and more today the world seems
to need people who at least try to listen. Before we can listen to
God I believe we have to listen to ourselves. Listening to
ourselves is one of the hardest things to do, partly because of
fear . . . we don't know what we're going to hear and we may
hear things that we'd rather not hear and if we hear them that
generally means that we have to do something about whatever
it is we hear and that may be more painful than we're prepared
to accept.

On his chosen prayer

It's by Brother Charles of Jesus who helped to found the Little
Brothers and Sisters of Jesus. I use it an awful lot, perhaps
every day, sometimes with my own personal changes in some
of the words.

It encourages me to abandon myself, to say to God, 'Here I
am to do your will, in your timing and in your way rather than
my own.' If I don't listen then I'll do things in my own way
and in my own time without the support, or obvious support,
of the mystery that we know as God.

God is love, so for me I'm abandoning myself to the mystery
of love. This love says to me that I'm nourished through the
love I receive from another individual person. Sometimes the
most wounded person is offering me a love through his or her
wounds. I'm quite convinced we're all born with the seed of
love and a Christian's function is to try and be a lover after the
manner of Christ and that means that we should go out and

meet God's people in every situation, whatever their faith or non-faith.

For me God is both male and female. We are told that he created us, male and female, and that we're made in his image. This must mean that God is both male and female. God is not only our ultimate father, but also our ultimate mother.

Prayer by Charles de Foucauld (1858–1916)

Father, I abandon myself into your hands.
Do with me what you will.
Whatever you may do, I thank you.
I am ready for all.
I accept all.
Let only your will be done in me
And in all your creatures.
I wish no more than this, O Lord.
Into your hands I commend my soul.
I offer it to you
With all the love of my heart,
For I love you, Lord,
And my brothers and sisters.
And so I need to give myself,
To surrender myself
Into your hands and theirs
Without reserve, with boundless confidence.
For you are my Father,
You are my Mother.
Amen.

•

THE VENERABLE TIMOTHY RAPHAEL, Archdeacon of Middlesex

On daily prayer

I've always found it a way of expressing how I feel . . . and how I am at a particular time. I don't often feel refreshed at the end of it and I certainly don't do it out of duty, but it's a way of actually sharing with God how I am at the moment and how things are: whether I'm feeling happy or sad, or tired or anxious. This is my valid prayer at this time, and to be able to express it, get it out of the system, if you like, and share it with someone, does make a difference.

On his chosen prayer

I've used it a lot over the last ten or fifteen years and I use it a lot both when I'm alone and with others because it's short and straightforward and uses mostly words of one syllable and it's a great expression of how we are.

It reminds us as well as God that we're his witnesses, and then it looks for cleansing from two things that really bother me. One is unbelief, I don't mean intellectual unbelief, but infidelity of spirit, just not being faithful to the God who calls us and who we have previously trusted in. It's breaking faith and I'm not speaking about those times when we sometimes wonder if there's a heaven or something like that which is what we all tend to do.

The other is sloth, you know that animal, three toes, hanging upside down in the jungle. That's how one so often is, just unable to do anything, paralysed by sloth.

Then the prayer asks that we should be filled with hope – which is the most vital quality needed today, I think – and it asks for zeal which is the antidote to sloth.

The best part of the prayer for me, though, is the last part which has four verbs, doing words. Someone once said that God is a verb and not a noun. I go for that. Doing things, getting on with our work, this is the first thing. Secondly the bearing, because all of us some of the time, and some people most of the time, have actually to be on the receiving end and can't do anything, and this is the suffering. And then there's the waiting, the expectancy, put in this prayer in old-fashioned terms of 'biding your time', in other words waiting and not being impatient. Then finally it speaks of 'seeing your glory' which is the ultimate vision for all of us of being with God and with one another.

Prayer

Father, you've called us to be your witnesses.
Cleanse us from unbelief and sloth,
And fill us with hope and zeal;
That we may do your work,
And bear your Cross,

And bide your time,
And see your Glory,
Through Christ our Lord.   Amen.

●

THE VERY REVEREND ALAN WEBSTER, former Dean of St Paul's Cathedral

On his chosen prayer

It's a blessing for those laying down office. It begins by saying that God rested on the seventh day and it's a hint that we should have more time than it's easy to have if you've been doing the kind of job that Margaret, my wife, has been doing for the Movement for the Ordination of Women, or that I've been doing as Dean of St Paul's, concerned with the central government of the Church of England and on many committees. So, the prayer says to me that I should look at my own agenda and not be cross if people ask if I'm not too busy at meetings and making decisions. It reminds me that having time available is a joyful and divine thing.

Then the prayer hints that we shouldn't think of God as Father, as the sort of Managing Director, in patriarchal terms. The church always looks so masculine and authoritative and this is challenged by the prayer which sees God as mother as well as father, and refers to God as 'she'.

I'm going to retire to Norwich where the first book in English was written by a woman whose name we don't know, but she lived by a church called St Julian's church, so she's called Julian of Norwich. She had a remarkable vision: she said that when we pray to God we should pray to God as our mother as well as our father, and when we think of our Lord Jesus Christ, we should think of him as our Lord but also in motherly terms, in feminine terms as well as masculine. She called her book *Revelations of Divine Love* because she believed that all that mattered is love. I often scurry to her book.

The prayer also speaks about being held in God's arms; this means a great deal to me. As Dean of St Paul's one is often criticised because one has to be up-front even if one isn't a very public kind of person. . . . I think I'm more shy and inward-looking than public, but you're inevitably criticised in news-papers and recently I saw a headline, 'Good riddance to the Dean'. Well, I think one just has to take these things. But when such things happen I remember that a great many people pray for St Paul's and pray for the church and pray for the Kingdom, including people outside the Christian religion, and I feel one is carried in people's arms, and these arms are really prayers. I see these prayers as a kind of web of good thoughts which surround the world – ultimately much tougher than the web of hostility or the web of competition which entangle our relationships. So I think that praying about being held in arms is not something abstract. It is for real and, though mysterious, yet intelligible because it means that there is a web of thinking which can bind humanity together, spun by the hidden Spirit.

From *All Desires Known*
Janet Morley

May the God who rested on the seventh day
to delight in all her creation
hold you in her arms
as you have held this work,
celebrate with us
the life that takes life from you,
and give you grace to let go
into a new freedom.   Amen.

This prayer was sent by Janet Morley as a retirement gift to the Dean and his wife, Margaret. It has since been published in *All Desires Known*, a collection of alternative collects and other prayers, by Janet Morley. The conversation was broadcast on the Saturday before the Dean went on pre-retirement leave.

•

FATIMA MERNISSI, sociologist and writer, researcher at the Centre for Scientific Research, Mohammed V University, Rabat, Morocco

On her chosen meditation

The words are those of Mimouna. Mimouna is a woman saint. We don't know exactly in what century she lived; probably it was the sixteenth century when religion played a very important political role against the colonisers – the Spanish and the Portuguese who invaded the northern coast of Africa. Of course we don't know for sure as, since she is a woman, she doesn't have a real historical profile, but she lives in people's memories.

Stories of the saints were a part of my oral education, an education which was mostly done by women. That's how I learnt about Mimouna. It was my grandmother who told me about Mimouna and about her very heretical and strange prayer, heretical by orthodox Islam standards. But surely Mimouna made a lot of sense for my grandmother, and she's made a lot of sense for me.

On her relationship to God

A lot of Muslims now, Muslim men, think that God and the Koran and all the sacred texts are their monopoly, and that women have no right to them. The relationship to God is evidently different in a country where God is monopolised and politicised as in theocracies, Muslim theocracies. It is very difficult when God is monopolised by the politicians for me to talk about a personal relationship with God. To do so would make it appear that I was submitting to the decisions of politicians about the kind of God they want to force on me.

For my grandmother, as for Mimouna – at least Mimouna as told to me by my grandmother – God was this space where the moment you are in it, you are totally capable of choosing any fate you want, any destiny. There is no limit to what you can do or what you can realise. There is no class, no limitations at all, no male or female conflicts. That's what God is to Mimouna. God gives you power to cut down hierarchies, to refuse them, to reject them.

I think that's what Mimouna's God and my grandmother's God is, and it makes God appealing. It makes the human being so powerful, no matter what the identity of that person is, and surely it does make the poor and the feeble and the weak totally omnipotent. I think that's the God I like.

Saying of Mimouna, Moroccan saint (sixteenth century)

Mimouna knows God,
and
God knows Mimouna.

GERALD SMITH, headmaster and founder of St Peter's School, Northampton

On the merits of a school prayer

I often tell the students that if in later life all their possessions are removed and they find themselves perhaps on a desert island, or even in prison for their principles, they must have something to hang on to. If they know this prayer, it's always something to fall back on because it covers so many facets of life.

I asked some of them the other day just what the prayer meant to them, and a variety of comments came in:

'God knows us well and sees us for what we are.'
'We shouldn't hide our feelings from God.'
'God sets the ideals, we must do our best.'
'God is watching and helping us at all times.'
'God knows how easy it is to be led into temptation.'

Most children seemed to feel that the prayer helps them to know and remember that God knows their feelings.

This is a school with children from various faiths. The prayer reminds them that we're all here living together for a certain period of time and that if we want to produce happiness for ourselves, we take the simple, straightforward way of being humble and sincere with each other, of respecting different ways of life from our own, and of respecting each other's religion. It teaches them to take an interest in the ancestral background of each other and to work and strive for a unity through the cleansing wind of reality, that is, through the Holy Spirit.

On God

A kind, loving, heavenly artist . . . the Creator. I see God as a kind of creative artist. He must surely be an artist, look at the trees, look even at a single blade of grass. I don't have to be a poet to know that I can't create that, only a marvellous artist can create it. All art breathes a kind of reality, all art develops our personality. Every single human being is different in one way or another and yet each single human being is similar to other human beings. We're all united in the Holy Spirit.

School prayer of St Peter's School, Northampton

O God, who knowest each one of us
Better than we know ourselves,
Who knowest how easy it is for us
To act and pose and pretend,
Send thy Holy Spirit and
Breathe into our lives
The cleansing wind of reality.
Take from us all sham, pretence and hypocrisy,
And make us humble and sincere,
Simple and straightforward;
For the sake of Jesus Christ our Lord.   Amen.

•

REVEREND DR DAVID RUSSELL, formerly General Secretary of the Baptist Union of Great Britain and Ireland, writer on the Old Testament and the Inter-Testamental books of the Bible

On his chosen meditation

The lines that I've chosen concern the relation of work with worship and that to me has been a very important factor all through my life. The lines remind me that you can worship God not only in your private devotions and not only in your public worship (and these two things are very important indeed), but you can worship God too by the work of your hands and by the work of your brains.

I'm reminded that Jesus himself not only worshipped God in the quiet places – the mountain tops and the desert – and not only in the synagogue and in the temple, but he glorified God with the hammer and the chisel and the saw. At least that's how I read my Gospel story. This impression was reinforced in me some little time ago when I visited Nazareth where Jesus himself was brought up. There's a Christian hospital there and in the hospital there's a chapel. It's an ordinary chapel – except for one thing. It has a communion table, or altar if you like, and this communion table is built in the shape of a carpenter's bench. It impressed on me that Jesus glorified God in what he did with his hands.

The lines also reflect attitudes which we tend to have to those who work with their hands. We're told in the Gospels that Jesus was a carpenter like his father before him. There were those in his own day who rather looked down their noses at him, as we would say, for that very reason. But the very fact that he was a carpenter has glorified this calling – because that's what it is – all through the centuries. I'm sure that a man or a woman can glorify God every bit as much with the plane or the saw or the typewriter as Jesus did by worshipping in the temple sabbath by sabbath.

There's a story which helps me to remember that God is very present in the workplace. It's the account of Brother Lawrence in his famous classic in devotion. Brother Lawrence was a monk who worked in a monastery and he tells us in his little book, *The Practice of the Presence of God*, that in the noise and clutter of his kitchen when many people were calling for many things at the same time, he could be aware of the presence of God every bit as much as he could be when he was on his knees at the blessed sacrament. How wonderful!

Meditation

Is not this the carpenter?[1]

Without them [craftsmen such as carpenters, painters, blacksmiths and potters], a city cannot be established. They keep stable the fabric of the world and their prayer is in the practice of their trade.[2]

[1] From the Gospel according to Mark, Chapter 6 verse 3
[2] From Ecclesiasticus in the Apocrypha, Chapter 38, verses 32 and 34

●

MATHOOR KRISHNAMURTI, Executive Director of the Institute of Indian Culture in London

On daily prayer

Our prayers are in general of two types: the personal prayers for one's own family, which are, one might say, the minor prayers; and then the more important prayers. We Hindus are taught to pray for the good of all humanity. We firmly believe, as the religion itself says, that God is in every being and that everybody should be happy and peaceful. Almost all our prayers are for universal good. That is how we are taught and that is how we pray. The major prayers in our daily lives are the prayers for all humanity.

As we grow older and older we realise how wise our ancestors were when they taught that if your neighbour is happy then you will be happy. Astonishing this insight is.

We also believe that our prayers will not fall on deaf ears. We firmly believe the vibrations will have an effect. That's why we put so much store on inter-religious prayers and inter-faith dialogue when thousands and thousands of people pray together for peace. We know that one day this peace will be there, one day those people who cause wars and destruction will realise that they are not right. Constant prayer has to be made; it is our dharma; it is our duty.

Guru Nanak, the great teacher of the Sikh religion, once was trying to save a scorpion which was caught in the currents of a river. Each time he tried to pull the scorpion from the river, the scorpion would bite his finger. Again he would try. Two or three times he got hold of the scorpion and two or three times the scorpion bit his finger. An onlooker said to him, 'Aren't you a stupid fellow. Why do you try to save the scorpion? Don't you know it's poisonous, it bites you?' Guru Nanak replied, 'Biting is its religion or nature. Saving is my religion, my dharma!'

So it's our duty to pray. We should not be despondent when we see violence everywhere. We should never stop praying.

Prayer from the *Rig Veda* (2000–3000 BC)

To live in peace, harmony, and to serve the cause of humanity,
   be united!
Speak in harmony;
Let our minds apprehend alike,
Common be our prayer.
Common be the end of our assembly,
Common be our resolution,
Common be our deliberations.
Alike be our feelings for our fellow beings,
Unified be our hearts.
Common be our intentions and perfect be our unity. Rigveda.

Why so? One may ask.

Because the world is one family.

Therefore, let noble thoughts
Come to us from every side.
Only then can we have peace,
Peace, and perfect peace.

●

FATHER MICHAEL SIMPSON, SJ, Catholic priest and Retreat Director at St Beuno's Centre of Spirituality in North Wales

On his chosen meditation

Some years ago I made a retreat in Canada. On the grounds of the retreat house there were wooden cabins which were given the name Poustinia. 'Poustinia' means 'desert place' in Russian but here refers to a state of spiritual solitude. It is also the name of the book from which my chosen passage comes.

I spent some days in one of these Poustinia during the retreat and I found that two questions were welling up within me. It was as if I was saying to Jesus, 'Lord, who are you, who are you for my life?' and 'Lord who am I, who really am I deep down?' The questions are seeking something deeper than simply theological facts about Jesus or biographical facts about my own life. I am asking about the reality of who Christ truly is and of who I truly am in the depth of my being, and I know that the answer to the question of who I am is intimately bound up with the question of who Jesus is. I see the mystery of my own life in the mystery of Jesus's life.

To go further I turned to the Gospels. My attention was led to a number of scenes where Jesus appears in a very human way, for instance when he washed the feet of his disciples. It came across to me that the important question is not so much whether Jesus is divine but whether we can really believe that God is what we find revealed and manifested in Jesus. When I look at the Gospels and see the humanness of Jesus, that humanness itself is a revelation of our God. I see who Jesus is, who God is, as a God who becomes poor with the poor, who takes on the form of the lost, the broken, the weak; the God who enters deeply into the pain of what it is to be human. And I see that my own call is in some way to share in that; that I have also got to be willing with Jesus to enter into the places of pain and brokenness in our world, in the lives of the men and women who are suffering so much.

The verse speaks of wisdom and that wisdom is a gift of God, when God through his Spirit touches our understanding, gives us deeper insights, helps us to see our human life from a divine perspective and not just out of our own human perspective.

I have a place where I pray each day. In front of me is an icon of Jesus and my Bible and a candle, and this is my own 'poustinia' within my room in the community where I live. But even more important than that, each one of us needs to create a 'poustinia', a place of solitude within our own hearts. However busy we are we all need some place of solitude, of withdrawal. The most important thing however is not exterior solitude or withdrawal, but a place deep within our hearts where we can find God and where we can find peace. It is there that we shall also find our own true self.

Poustinia from *Christian Spirituality of the East for Western Man*
Catherine de Hueck Doherty

Listen to yourself, so as to find the path to God within the frail
    walls of your humanness,
Listen to yourself, for it is you alone who will lead yourself to
    him, or away from him.
Listen to yourself, listen to God, when you have led yourself
    to him.
Listen well, for if you hear his voice
you will be wise with the wisdom of the Lord;
and then you will be able to hear the voice of men,
not as a surging sea, or as a mob.
But each man's speech is his own,
a treasure given to you beyond all expectations,
because you led yourself to him and listened to his voice.

•

MARGARET HEBBLETHWAITE, writer

On her chosen meditation

The passage reflects a kind of Christian ministry in which you're not someone high up who's doing things for the benefit of people at the bottom, but you're trying to be with the people at the bottom and identify with them, not having privileges beyond what they have. You're trying to understand what it means to be in their position, and to facilitate from the bottom. It's very difficult and perhaps the best way of explaining the difficulties is through examples.

I was involved in ministry in a prison and I became very aware that in the prison ministry there were two very different ways of doing things. One was to be a Chaplain with authority who had the ear of the Governor and wore a Chaplain's uniform and sat on committees hoping to influence the committees for the good of the prisoners. That's one model of ministry.

Because of this passage, that wasn't the way I wanted to do things. Once you start not wearing uniform and not drinking coffee in the Officer's Mess, and instead you start being with the prisoners, and not taking on other privileges, that's a wholly different way of doing things and it's a very difficult way to go. It doesn't mean that you identify with everything the prisoners stand for. I would sometimes say to the prisoners that I thought things they'd done or were planning to do were wrong. But I could say that to them and they would accept it because I was on their level.

There are times when I've felt very isolated and when I've questioned whether my way of ministering is Christian, and I think this passage is something that I hold on to. If my conscience is right in terms of this passage, then I'm not too deeply disturbed.

I think the key to it from the Christian gospel is in the idea of Incarnation, the idea that God saved us, not from above, but by becoming one with us and going through the suffering with us; by being born in poverty, by having friends who were sinners, sexual sinners often, and in the end by dying a criminal's death.

Based on an extract from an article in *Jesuits and Friends*

We try to place special emphasis on being with rather than doing for. We want our presence among the poor to be one of sharing with them, of accompaniment, of walking together along the same path. In so far as possible, we want to feel what they have felt, suffer as they have, share the same hopes and aspirations, see the world through their eyes. We ourselves would like to become one with the poor and the oppressed peoples so that, all together, we can begin the search for a new life.

●

BISHOP KALISTOS WARE, Bishop of the Greek Orthodox Church, Lecturer in Eastern Orthodox Studies at Oxford University and writer

On Orthodoxy

I first came to know the Orthodox Church when I was seventeen. What attracted me in the beginning was the prayers, the worship. After a time I found out more; what the Orthodox teach, what they believe. The more I learnt, the more I felt that this was exactly what I believed already, only I'd never heard it so well expressed. So I came to feel increasingly at home in Orthodoxy. It was a gradual process, it took about six years before I actually joined the Orthodox Church.

On daily prayer

I'm a member of the monastery of St John on the island of Patmos. I try to go there every year. When I'm in the monastery, then we have long services starting at around 2.30 in the morning; and so I have plenty of time for full liturgical services in church. But here in Oxford, I have to do my job teaching, and I have to try and help in parish work, and that doesn't give me much time on weekdays for elaborate services. So here I need to have a form of prayer that will be quite simple. I need a form of prayer that will help me to preserve a certain stillness in the midst of all my activities. If all through the day you're continually talking, meeting different people, you need also to have the element of silence, inner listening, and you need a form of prayer that will help you with that.

On his chosen prayer

The Jesus Prayer is short. It is an invocation to the Lord Jesus Christ, and we speak of him as Son of God. We ask him to have mercy. Some people think the words 'have mercy' are a little gloomy, somewhat sombre. I don't find the word 'mercy' gloomy at all, I find it a word full of hope. For me the word 'mercy' means the love of God poured out to heal. So when I say to God 'have mercy', I come before him in my brokenness, but also knowing that God affirms me, that God heals and that God gives me life. When I say, 'have mercy', I'm thinking chiefly of the power of God coming out to make me and all of us whole.

This is a prayer that we Orthodox may say during our special prayer time. We repeat it a number of times, not mechanically but concentrating on the inner meaning. It's a prayer which helps to produce precisely the attitude of listening that I mentioned earlier. Prayer shouldn't be just us talking to God, we should also be listening to the voice of the Holy Spirit, the voice of Christ in our own heart. This prayer being so short and so simple, even though it is a prayer in words, helps us to reach out beyond words into silence.

Then I also use it during the day, in all the odd moments that would otherwise be wasted. At moments of tension and difficulty, or anxiety or irritation, I say this prayer inwardly to help to centre me. So it's both a prayer of quietness, to be said in prayer time, and a prayer for use throughout the day, bringing the spirit of Christ into all our daily tasks.

The Jesus Prayer (seventh century AD)

Lord, Jesus Christ, Son of God,
Have mercy on us.

•

THELMA BAILEY, writer who runs a ministry for those in prison

On fear

Just recently I had a very bad time physically when I just didn't know what was going to happen next, but during that time the Lord spoke to me very clearly. There's a phrase which says that 'perfect love casts out fear', and God's love did cast out all my fear. There was a wonderful sense of joy and freedom.

The other occasion was the first time I entered a prison to give my very first talk in that situation. I felt personally very inadequate but I was able to do it with God's strength and help. He was with me in a very real way and strengthened me through that time and I was filled with a tremendous sense of love which didn't come from me at all but from the Holy Spirit. There's also this longing to just do more and more with the prisoners, to share with them the fact that God can use their dark situations and bring them into the light.

When panic seizes me I try to remember that the Lord is there at all times, even in the dark times. There was one occasion when I was in Southampton General Hospital and I was feeling very ill indeed and it was a very gloomy night with lots of clouds and the moon kept disappearing. It was dark and horrible and all of a sudden the moon re-appeared and that reminded me of the verse where it says, 'Nevertheless that time of darkness and despair will not go on for ever.' I've always remembered that when I have a difficult time.

On her meditation

I first heard this passage quite some time ago, but until recently it didn't have the significance for me that it does now. A short time ago I had a very vivid prayer picture during my prayer time, a picture of going out into the darkness and God's hand was literally leading me out into a desert, a place of peace, and this ties up very beautifully with the passage.

I've had a wasting disease almost all of my life, but I don't think there was ever a time when I felt angry at God. Somebody wrote to me and said that when God makes a mistake he makes up for it by doing this, that and the other. God doesn't make mistakes and we can be used by him in every situation if we are willing to be open to the leading of his Spirit.

He gives us the strength to cope with all situations. I try to remember that Christ suffered too; he's with us right the way through; he knows what it's like. The more disabled I've become, the more evident that truth has been to me.

From *The Desert, 1908*
M. Louise Haskins (1875–1957)

I said to the man who stood at the gate of the year,
Give me a light that I may tread safely into the unknown.
And he replied – Go out into the darkness and put thine hand
  into the hand of God.
That shall be to thee better than a light and safer than a known
  way.

•

REVEREND DEREK RICHARDS, Rector of Llandudno

On his relationship with God

I question God frequently, twice, three times a day, with all sorts of things that happen or don't happen during the day. One keeps on saying, 'Why has this happened to me?' when things go wrong or one is lonely; but when things go right one very rarely remembers to ask why this has happened. One strives for a balance between these two.

I once lost my faith, for about a week, and that was the most horrifying and dreadful time. I went to my Bishop and said that I could not continue because of the lack of faith. We talked for a long time and at the end I asked him to bless me which he did, and I could feel the faith coming straight back into me as he blessed me. It didn't solve a lot of problems, but the faith came back and that was the most important thing. One wavers occasionally; I often look at people in the pews and think, 'My goodness, what are you doing here and what am I doing here too for that matter?' – but we know what we're doing, we're worshipping God. It is the worship of God which is so important and certainly the way one worships him.

The thing that threatens my faith most is loneliness. I think that is the dragon in my life. But one can take one's loneliness to Jesus Christ and say, 'You know exactly what it's like. You know what it's like to be very often without friends, to be cut

52

off, as it were.' So one can take all one's joys and one's sorrows and everything that happens to Jesus and indeed, one offers them at the Eucharist every day. We're fortunate here to celebrate the Eucharist daily.

I'm not what I call a sort of hallelujah hand-shake worshipper. My form of worship is ordered and done with as much dignity and peace as possible. Indeed, in this parish recently we've tried to introduce much more silence into our worship, to do things more slowly, to bring the words to people and give them time to reflect on their meaning. We're finding already that these silences and this calmness are having an enriching effect on our worship.

Prayer by Alfred Doerffler

Out of the depths of my misery and distress I cry to Thee, gracious Father in Christ Jesus. Lift me out of my suffering and anxiety. I need Thee from hour to hour to keep my faith strong and my hopes high. I look through a glass darkly, at the present moment, and tearfully ask: Why has this happened to me? Give me the grace to believe that Thy love to sinful and helpless me is as boundless as the ocean. Forgive me all my sins, ease my pain, and restore me to health. Hear my prayers for Jesus' sake.   Amen.

•

JAMES ROOSE-EVANS, founder of Hampstead Theatre, theatrical director, writer and Anglican priest

On his chosen prayer

One of my favourite prayers is the prayer of the night office, Compline. The prayer falls into three sections for me.

First there's the phrase, 'visit this house, we beseech thee, O Lord'. It's like an invitation to a guest to come and live with one. The house is also a very potent image for me. Whether one lives in a bed-sitter, a cottage or a council house, there's the feeling of a roof over one's head giving protection, the image of a fire by which one can warm oneself, a table where one can share food and celebrate, windows that look out on to the world and there's a door where one can welcome people, but also shut out the outside world. One is very vulnerable and yet

53

safe within one's home.

But the prayer goes on to say, 'drive far from it all snares of the enemy'. I think we have a great need to put almost a magic circle round us. We ask God to draw this circle round us, to bless us in our homes, so that we may be safe. I like the imagery of snares of the enemy. We need to be much more aware of the power of darkness in the world today, not only the darkness of our own negative thoughts and destructive emotions, but the very objective power of evil – what St Paul calls the principalities and powers of darkness – and we need God to protect us from this darkness, because it can infiltrate through the windows, through the doors of our interior house as it were, and become very destructive indeed. Therefore the prayer goes on to ask, 'may thy holy angels dwell herein'.

People have difficulties with angels nowadays. I don't have any difficulty at all. I think people tend to think of white robes and wings. Those are only pictures to enable us to realise that there are presences that move with tremendous speed, presences with the brilliance of light, because they come to us from God. These angels may come to us in dreams, or on suddenly waking up with a strong intuition about something. I also believe that each one of us has a guardian angel appointed to look after us. It's very important therefore that this prayer asks God to bless this house, to keep far from me all powers of darkness and to put around me the presences of his angels.

Then the prayer ends, 'may thy blessing be always upon us'. That's not only in this life but in eternity . . . to be always in the presence of the blessing of God.

The image of God the Protector is very strong with me. We each need a centre in our lives, and home is my centre. Home is also where God is and if God is in the home of my heart then I'm eternally protected, wherever I move, whether I'm in great danger or die suddenly in a car crash, I'm surrounded and supported by God's blessing and by the presence of his angels. There's nothing to fear.

Prayer from the night office of Compline

Visit this house, we beseech thee, O Lord, and drive far from it all the snares of the enemy. May thy holy angels dwell herein, and may thy blessing be always upon us. Through Christ our Lord. Amen.

MICHAEL TAYLOR, Director of Christian Aid

On his meditation

In this poem, which I wrote for our House magazine, you see in the cradle the helpless child who can do very little for himself, and then you see the same child grown to be a man and helpless on a Cross.

There's been one part of Christian tradition, I suppose, that thought if Jesus had really decided to come down from the Cross he could have done so. But there's another tradition, and perhaps the stronger one, that knows that he really wanted to get off the Cross like any human being would, but being genuinely human he couldn't. So there's a helplessness about Christ that is both redemptive and healing and creative. That helplessness, however, has to be compared very carefully with the helplessness of the poor.

Now there's a quite wrong sense of saying, 'Those poor people are helpless' – because they're very, very skilful, very resourceful, very active people. But there is a sense that many of the poor have very little control over what happens to them. Now that's a helplessness that they don't choose and they don't want, and it's very different from the helplessness of the Christ child where Christian faith believes that God in a sense has chosen that helplessness. So one kind of helplessness is redemptive and creative but the other kind very definitely is not.

I also suggest in the poem that suffering doesn't always save. In our work there's a lot of talk about the idea of the Gospel and the poor. It's widely accepted that the Gospel is certainly for the poor, but there's another idea that creeps in which I think is equally valid, but has to be handled quite carefully. It's actually those poor people who, by their resilience and their courage, give us back our faith in a way which we could never give it to them; so I find something very valid in saying I receive my salvation from the poor. But it's easy to slip over from recognising that to beginning to romanticise about the poor (who can be difficult people as we can be), and to romanticise about their suffering. You have to be very careful not to edge towards calling what is clearly evil, good – the suffering they have to endure, the hunger, the deprivation, the oppression, the lack of power, the lack of ability to decide what happens to them. You have to be very careful not to start saying that somehow that suffering is part of what saves them, instead of recognising that their condition is something which we should be absolutely against.

Poem by Michael Taylor

Helpless God, as child and crucified,
Laid in a cradle and cradled on a cross,
Help us discern in your submission
Not weakness but the passionate work of love.

You tell us you are poor in every age
Naked, hungry and without a home.

Help us in your poor cradle of today
To see what is of you and what is not:
That suffering does not often save,
Or helplessness redeem our sorry lives,
And so forbid us sing where we should weep.

Yet come to us and all of ours,
O child of Mary and of God,
In all the poor who saw you first,
And laughed with you and heard you well,
And now run back from nowhere with their news
To plant their seeds of hope in our dry ground.

•

JESSYE NORMAN, opera singer. Miss Norman grew up in a Baptist family in Georgia, USA, and describes herself as never having been without a religious faith.

On her chosen prayer

I think this prayer means a lot to me because it has to do with singing and it sets us at one with nature. That's the way that I feel about prayer in general and about life quite specifically. I seem to feel at ease, at my best and at my most spiritual when I'm walking in nature, in the forest where you can't see a house for miles. There I can concentrate on thoughts about my life, friendships, my work and so on. These things I can really do only when walking quite quietly, whether with a group of people or alone, as then I have this sense of oneness with nature. In cities I rely on city parks and in a place like London this is easy.

I found the prayer in a wonderful book, a book which tells of ceremonies of native Americans, ceremonies which have been going on for centuries and are still going on – in very small communities I'm afraid now.

In the prayer one is standing and one is upright and one is looking upward and not on one's knees with head bent and with the weight of the world on one's shoulders. This posture for praying is another thing which attracted me to this prayer. It gives me a feeling of positiveness in life. The prayer is one of celebration.

It speaks about the end of life and says that life, its beginning and end, is determined by a force that we can sense and feel, but cannot see. This force will determine when my time on earth should be finished. When this happens I would like it to be pleasant and a wonderful experience. I would certainly want my end to be the responsibility of someone else. I've had some friends who have ended their own lives. I think we probably all have known people who have done that, but I find that I'm angry at them for having done it. I'm angry that they've taken this power into their own hands at that moment. Of course life is very difficult and extremely complicated for most of us but I think that death is something that we have to allow to happen rather than something that we make happen. That's my very simple feeling about it all.

Translation by Hartley Burr Alexander of a North American Indian prayer, 'Last Song'
From I Send a Voice *by Evelyn Eaton*

Let it be beautiful
When I sing the last song.
Let it be day.
I would stand upon my two feet, singing,
I would look upward with my eyes, singing,
I would have the winds to envelop my body,
I would have the sun to shine upon my body.
Let it be beautiful,
When Thou wouldst slay me, O Shining One.
Let it be day when I sing the last song.

JOHN FIGUEROA, Jamaican poet and academic

On his thoughts on writing this prayer

The old manuals, which are perhaps more correct than we liberated people think, used to say, 'Prayer is the raising of the heart and mind to God,' and whenever I have to do bidding prayers in church, or volunteer to do them, I try to bring our minds and our hearts to contemplate certain things. We should realise much more than we do that to contemplate, to think, to consider does not mean withdrawal from active life. It does for some people, but it doesn't need to.

I'm also a little bit tired – in the political world and even in the academic world – of the noise-makers who are always shouting. We need much more contemplation and consideration and stillness. Obviously one has to complain about certain things and one has to make a noise about certain things, but if one makes a noise about everything then obviously the noise doesn't matter even as noise. I think my reference in the prayer to 'idiotic whirl' had to do with too quick a reaction and perhaps with too much of an expectation of perfection.

On prayer in general

If you read St John of the Cross or Thomas Aquinas they're very strong on saying that prayer is not a matter of asking for things. Aquinas even says, 'We use language with God, not to manifest our thoughts to him, for he is the searcher of hearts, but to induce reverence in ourselves and in others.'

I find nature helpful to my prayers at times. I was very much made aware of how troublesome nature can be from being in hurricanes and earthquakes, but on the other hand there are peaceful moments – certain combinations of light at sunsets in the tropics, or morning star in the winter countries, and something just shines out. Then one seems to feel that there is more there than one thought of and I think an awareness of this can come to all of us. If we don't try to do that in the modern world there's no way we're going to have any inner life.

Prayer written by John Figueroa

O God, whose prophet found you
    not in the earthquake
    nor in the hurricane,

Who shouted at Job
  be still and know that I am your God,

Teach us to listen to the gentle breeze,
  and not to be misled by the thunderers.
Teach us to care . . . for others,
    for their sufferings and their successes,
    and not to care for ourselves
    and our petty problems,
    and minor triumphs.

And when the world quakes
  and is in an idiotic whirl,

Teach us to care and not to care,

'Teach us to sit still.'

•

THE RIGHT REVEREND JAMES TAKASHI YASHIRO, Bishop of Kita Kanto, Japan

On his chosen prayer

I have one prayer which is particularly dear to me. It is a prayer about peace. Peace is my deepest concern.

What we usually mean by peace is something maintained by physical power, by force; this is the peace that the world can give. But the peace for which we pray is something which the world cannot give. Let me give you an example of this.

In my diocese, to the north of Tokyo, there is a town called Kusatsu, famous for its hot springs. This place is also famous for its leper colony which was started by an English missionary woman, Miss Cornwall Leigh, about seventy-five years ago. In those days leprosy was like AIDS today, abhorred by all, and when people got sick with leprosy they were disowned and expelled from their community. So many of them came to Kusatsu because they thought the hot springs were good for the disease. The townspeople of Kusatsu didn't want to have anything to do with the lepers and it was this missionary woman, Miss Cornwall Leigh, who decided to give all her money and everything she had to found a colony with a chapel for them. Many of them became Christians, Anglicans.

Then the war came and Miss Leigh was an enemy person for the Japanese, but for the lepers she was not an enemy. The peace sustained by political and physical forces was broken by the outbreak of war but the peace given by this missionary who gave everything she had was sustained. When she died, even though the war was still going on, the mother of the present Emperor sent flowers and she was awarded a special medal.

So, in the long run, the peace which presupposes sacrifice or hardship or even self-denial will endure much longer than the peace which is sustained by the physical forces of this world.

Prayer for the 4th Sunday before Easter, from the Anglican Alternative Service Book, 1980

Almighty God, whose most dear Son went not to joy, but first he suffered pain and entered not into glory before he was crucified; mercifully grant that we, walking in the way of the Cross, may find it none other than the way of life and peace, through Jesus Christ our Lord.   Amen.

•

ELIZABETH BRIERE, Secretary, the Fellowship of St Alban and St Sergius – a group which exists to foster contact and understanding between Orthodox and other Christian churches. She is a member of the Patriarchal Russian Orthodox Church.

On her journey in prayer

I feel I'm a beginner; in fact, it would be proud to say even 'a beginner' for actually I don't feel I have begun. Perhaps because of that, liturgical prayer is very important to me because I feel that even with my experience I am carried along by the prayer of the church . . . both the people who surround me and all the other members of the church throughout history. This is a way in which I feel I can start learning to pray.

On her chosen prayer

It's a prayer which belongs to Pentecost and is also used at other times of the year. It speaks in a very personal and very direct way to Christ. Christ is known to us through the Holy

Spirit. There is a kind of intimacy in this prayer which we don't often find in other prayers. An intimacy in the way it addresses Jesus directly, saying 'Give swift and sure comfort to thy servant.'

It likens our closeness to Christ, the closeness that we wish to have with him, with the contact that the apostles had. In other words it's a very vivid way of bridging the gap between those who are historically with him and us.

A thought that I always find particularly moving is the amazing paradox, the contrast between the power of God, that he is almighty, and the fact that he comes to us. This paradox is expressed so vividly in the prayer when we say, 'Draw near to us, draw near, thou who art everywhere.' This is something that we're very aware of at Easter, something that we find in the light of the resurrection: that we are so close to God, God who is almighty, God who has trampled down death, who has conquered death. This is something the resurrection means to us. We have no fear for he who is everywhere, he who is all powerful, is near to us as well.

I really do feel that every liturgical experience of the resurrection is a real experience of resurrection. Year by year, living this liturgically I become more and more convinced that when I say, 'Christ is risen', I mean it.

Prayer by St Romanos the Melodist, from the liturgy of the Russian Orthodox Church

Give swift and sure comfort to thy servants, O Jesus, when our spirit is cast down within us.

Do not depart from our souls in our sorrows, do not be far from our thoughts in times of trouble, but go before us always.

Draw near to us, draw near, thou who art everywhere. And as thou art always with thine apostles, so also in thy mercy unite thyself to those who long for thee, that with one accord we may sing thy praise and glorify thine all Holy Spirit.

•

DAVID BEDFORD, Director of Y-Care International, the world development wing of the Young Men's Christian Association

The story of how the prayer came about

I wrote to the Reverend Dr Donald English and asked him to write a prayer for hostages for us. This was mainly because of the personal friendship I have with Terry Waite and also the working relationship with him as he's the Honorary Chairman of Y-Care. While Terry is away from us we wanted to write to the churches and to send them a prayer which perhaps both publicly and privately they could offer not only for Terry but for all the other hostages.

On hostage taking

Perhaps because Terry Waite is our Honorary Chairman we at Y-Care have been looking at the subject of hostage taking for some time. Terry Waite sees hostage taking as a response to the sort of world in which we live. He always implores us to ask why people take hostages, and he believes it's a direct response to some of the unfairnesses in the world. It's never right, but it's a response to oppression and poverty and persecution.

On the prayer

It seems to sum up for me the terrible strain, the terrible suffering which Terry and the others must be going through at the moment. It asks God to give grace to hostages during their time of suffering and the prayer outlines loneliness and turbulence, depression and hardship as some of the problems which are obviously facing them. Then, it says, 'When they are tempted to doubt even their own worth, may they know how much they matter to you and to us', and I'm sure that if through prayer somehow we can help the hostages to understand that they are loved by God and they are thought of by those of us left behind, then this is very important.

The other thing in the prayer which impresses me is when it says, 'In the soil of their suffering may the seeds of a better world be planted.' Again, I think of Terry. There he is, a tremendous symbol of hope for the world, and I think that possibly in the soil of his suffering the seeds of a better world are being laid.

On faith

Sometimes when you're faced by dreadful situations your faith is strengthened. If anything, that's happening to me. I know that one day my friend will come back and I think he will tell us about how his faith has been strengthened as well.

Prayer for hostages

Give grace, O Lord, to those held hostage at this time.
When loneliness envelops them, may they sense your
    presence.
When turbulence surrounds them, may they have inner peace.
When depression threatens them, may they find renewed
    hope.
When hardship burdens them, may they receive new strength.
When they are tempted to doubt even their own worth,
May they know how much they matter to you, and to us.
In the soil of their suffering may the seeds of a better world be
    planted.
We ask our prayers in the name of Him who, for their sake and
    ours, died and was raised,
Even Jesus Christ, our Lord.   Amen.

This prayer was commissioned by Y-Care, and written by the Reverend Dr Donald English.

•

RONALD BLYTHE, writer and Anglican lay reader

On Jesus Christ, his humanity and divinity

The Christ who walked about on earth is immensely real to me. He's so vivid, walking about the countryside, telling all those country stories, and the anger and the happiness and the meals. . . . I haven't found a problem between this human Jesus Christ and the divine Christ but I frequently meet people who do find this difficult. I always try and explain that it is his humanity which makes his divinity so exciting. It is the fact that he must have experienced every human experience that makes him so accessible to us. It is the fact that he had friends and he got tired and he quarrelled and was terribly moved by the new temple at Jerusalem, knowing that it couldn't last very long, that makes him recognisable. I find all this profoundly spiritual.

On the 'knowing and not knowing' of Christ's love

It's a great comfort not to know sometimes . . . to know that some knowledge is beyond our knowing. It's so honest. Even the great writers like St Paul couldn't express it. St Paul knew things and yet he didn't know. This mystery is so important in the faith.

On his prayer, taken from St Paul's letter to the Ephesians

Paul must have been near death. The prison letters have come out of a great humanity. I sometimes think of him, walking about before he was caught, walking in Asia Minor, all those great distances. Now he's trapped and he's got one or two people with him, those loyal people who stayed with him all the time. And then he writes these amazing words. They're so magnificent. You feel that he's got to tell people, perhaps well educated people, how wonderful Christianity really is, and he does it in the finest, most marvellous language. Indeed, he reaches the heights of genius in some of the writings in the letter to the Ephesians about prayer. . . .

He manages to put the illimitability of Christ's love into a language . . . it's such a great comfort to know it. Often, even in religious circumstances, one feels limitation and one meets limitation in theology . . . then suddenly one reads St Paul and one moves into another atmosphere altogether. This is what Christ really is, this illimitable Christ whom St Paul understands. I like to put some of his words into the first person.

From St Paul to the Ephesians, Chapter 3, verses 14–19

With this in mind, then, I kneel in prayer to the Father, from whom every family in heaven and on earth takes its name, that out of the treasures of his glory he may grant me strength and power through his Spirit in my inner being, that through faith Christ may dwell in my heart in love. With deep roots and firm foundations, may I be strong to grasp, with all God's people, what is the breadth and length and height and depth of the love of Christ, and to know it, though it is beyond knowledge. So may I attain to fullness of being, the fullness of God himself.

MICHELLE GUINNESS, writer and broadcaster who describes herself as 'Jewish Christian'

On her chosen prayer

It's a very visual passage. Julian (of Norwich) is in prayer. She's contemplating. She holds out the palm of her hand and she sees a tiny hazelnut lying on the palm of her hand. That's a very visual image. I dream in technicolour, so I like to pray in technicolour as well. I like to be able to see what I'm praying.

I think we all have a tendency to see the universe as being vast and we slot God into our scheme of things. I realised in this prayer that if the world is that tiny hazelnut, if that is how God sees it, then we are what is tiny and he fits us into his scheme of things. It was a complete reversal of how I saw God. It was quite shattering for me. At the same time I began to think, well, if the world was like that to God, what did it mean to Christ to come and be in this world and it seemed to me that probably the nearest equivalent was for a human being to become a goldfish and swim round in a goldfish bowl.

On prayer in general

I'm a great activist. I'm not somebody who finds prayer easy or to live in an attitude of communion with God. I just want to be up and doing all the time and there are many demands on my time with two small children. Indeed, it's sometimes hard to even think two sentences without being interrupted. That's why I like to have pictures in my mind. It's lovely to be able to go back to that picture and to feel that sense of the protection of God.

On living the Scriptures

Every year when we have the Passover together I feel as if it was my ancestors there in Egypt. I actually feel I was there myself. I know what it was like to be a slave in Egypt. I feel that sense of history as a Jew, and as a Christian too I'm beginning to learn that and I feel that's important. There's a lovely sense of time not just being for today. It goes on forever and ever. It's frightening and yet it's very wonderful too.

From *Revelations of Divine Love*
Julian of Norwich (fourteenth century)

And God showed me more, a little thing, the size of a hazelnut on the palm of my hand, round like a ball. I looked at it thoughtfully and wondered, 'What is this?' And the answer came, 'It is all that is made.' I marvelled that it continued to exist and did not suddenly disintegrate. It was so small, and again my mind supplied the answer. 'It exists both now and forever because God loves it. In short, everything owes its existence to the love of God.'

•

FATHER GERRY HUGHES, SJ, a priest and writer

On his choice of prayer

The words re-echo so much of St Paul and of St Ignatius, the founder of the Jesuits, that the Spirit of God is the spirit of all human beings and this Spirit expresses itself/herself/himself in different ways in different people, but it's the same Spirit.

It re-echoes a lot of the Christian mystics . . . the staggering sentence of St Catherine of Genoa, a sentence that begins, 'My God is me.' Something that sounds absolutely blasphemous. But then she goes on and says, 'Nor do I recognise any other me except my God himself.' Now that is a profound statement, and this prayer expresses that. Therefore when things get critical for me, for example when I'm afraid, I'm anxious, I'm fearful, I ask 'Who am I?' The answer? 'My God is me, nor do I recognise any other me except my God himself.' Then I begin to realise that a lot of my fears are about my private kingdom. They're fears which come out of my imagination, which imagines me as utterly separate from God, whereas my 'me' is God, and I don't want to recognise any other 'me', therefore the 'me' which is causing all this anxiety I can let drop, because there is God himself – and one can experience some measure of peace doing this.

On identity

The most difficult thing for all of us is to get rid of our own egoism. We require identity, that's important. There must be an 'I'. But the parameters of the 'I' need to be stretched out to infinity. They need to be stretched and they need in a way to be dissolved, to be done away with. What's involved is a discovery of the real 'I'.

There's a lovely second-century homily by an anonymous author, and it imagines Christ going down to hell after the crucifixion and he knocks at the door of Hell and calls out to Adam, 'Adam, arise, come forth. Henceforth you and I are one undivided person.' So it's deep in Christianity that our real identity is ultimately with God. And that is why we have such problems with our identity. We never know who we are and it's a very good thing that we don't, because otherwise we'd have the solution to God and if we had the solution to God he wouldn't be God anymore. It's good that we're puzzled.

God's Life Within, prayer by Tukarum (1608–49), an Indian peasant mystic

Take, Lord, unto Thyself,
My sense of self: and let it vanish utterly:

Take, Lord, my life,
Live thou Thy life through me:

I live no longer, Lord,
But in me now
Thou livest:

Aye, between Thee and me, my God,
There is no longer room for 'I' and 'mine'.

●

**SIR CLAUS MOSER, Warden of Wadham College,
Oxford, Vice-Chairman N. M. Rothschild & Sons Ltd, and
former Chairman, Royal Opera House, Covent Garden**

On being Jewish

I grew up as a Reform Jew in Berlin, I'm not Orthodox. I came from a typical Berlin Jewish family. We left Berlin in 1936 because of Hitler and came to Britain and my family have had a wonderful life here ever since.

As the years have gone on, being Jewish has meant more and more to me, not exactly in a religious sense – although it's a difficult distinction that – but being Jewish in the sense of having a commitment. The word commitment is one that I come back to again and again. It's a feeling that having had the Holocaust, the greatest horror of all time in the 1930s, and having survived it, one cannot be a passive Jew. Lots of people have ceased to be Jews, they've been confirmed into other religions. That's fine, that's their decision, that's a positive religious decision. But, if one remains a Jew as I've done, to be inactive is not acceptable. At least, that's what I think. As the years have gone by I've felt increasingly that what I want is not just to be a Jew and to be proud of being a Jew, but I want to commit myself in some way because of being a Jew.

Each one of us has his own way. I work very hard, or as hard as I can, for the Central British Fund for World Jewish Refugees. That, after all, is the organisation that helped a lot of us out from Germany and Austria in the 1930s. We help thousands of survivors of the Holocaust now. The other thing is this. Supposing one has neither money nor time nor opportunity, then the very least one can do is to think about the Holocaust. If one is a Jew who survived where millions and millions and millions of Jews perished, one simply cannot allow a week to pass without giving it some thought, without perhaps talking to others, educating children . . . you know the ignorance can be amazing. It's always a commitment to something one believes in and one cares about, a commitment that's become a central part of one's life.

When I think of the Holocaust there's a never-ending sense of horror. But there's also a more positive emotion and that is a determination that it just must not happen again. Any sign I see of intolerance; intolerance of minorities whether it be Jews or coloured people or any ethnic group or any particular believing group, any intolerance or injustice I see, I just cannot be comfortable, I must speak out. This is the most important emotion in me when I remember.

On his choice of meditation

It's a rather famous saying of a great man. He was Pastor Niemöller. He was a Christian and he preached in a church in Berlin which is about ten minutes from where I grew up. He spoke out against the Nazis and then ultimately became their victim.

Words of Pastor Martin Niemöller (1892–1984)

First they came for the Jews and I did not speak out, because I was not a Jew. Then they came for the communists and I did not speak out, because I was not a communist. Then they came for the trade unionists and I did not speak out, because I was not a trade unionist. And then they came for me, and there was no one left to speak out for me.

•

KERENA MERCHANT, researcher, BBC Television, Religious Programmes Department

On her chosen prayer

I think that one of the most difficult things to do is to break down the barriers of self. This prayer helps me to do this. In the first part of the prayer, 'Make me a channel of your peace', the ways you should work for God are described, and it's very idealistic. The second part of the prayer gives us ways to help us break down the barriers of self.

I'm deaf, I have a disability and I get very frustrated. It's very easy at times for me to feel sorry for myself. I feel like saying to people, 'You know, I can't understand what you're saying, I'm deaf and you're going to have to speak slowly and clearly. I hate you for not making the effort.' But then I have to remember that that person is struggling just as much as me to communicate, to try and understand me. At moments like this I try to think of the words of St Francis and say to myself, 'Look, come on, let's be cool, let's be calm, let's communicate together.' Now, maybe because I have a communication disability, the whole prayer to me is a story of opening up a two-way communication, even a three-way one; between God, the individual and the rest of humanity.

On God

My picture of God is in a way a Muslim one because I don't have a language to describe God. God's very all-embracing. I feel that we sit here and we wait on God.

I don't think anybody's faith is very constant . . . if they say it is, it's not very real. I used to be an atheist because I absolutely resented God because I was born deaf. I felt I was missing out on a very beautiful part of creation and I thought the Creator had a warped sense of humour to make me deaf. I absolutely resented that Creator. But then, I think in a way I was putting up the barriers of self and I wasn't opening up to the Creator in the way that this prayer is asking you to. It was only when I began to reduce the barriers of self and see the suffering of other people and see that there was a God who was very much in the suffering, that I began to appreciate God.

In a way I'm very grateful for the doubt. I think so many people go about with a blind understanding of God, and what you need is a faith that's made stronger through doubt. To me God's like a plant. He sort of grows in you, and if the roots grow deep, through a sort of struggle to come to terms with the environment, then that plant is a very strong plant.

Prayer of St Francis of Assisi (1181–1226)

Lord, make me a channel of your peace.
Where there is hatred, let me sow your love;
Where there is injury, your pardon, Lord;
Where there is doubt, true faith in you;
Where there is despair, hope;
Where there is darkness, light;
Where there is sadness, joy.
O divine Master, Grant that I may not so much seek
To be consoled, as to console,
To be understood, as to understand,
To be loved, as to love with all my soul.

●

FATHER MICHAEL CAMPBELL JOHNSTON, SJ,
Provincial, British Province of the Society of Jesus

On his chosen passage

The main thing that reaches through to me is that when we're considering how to act and what to do, we should weigh up our decisions in the light of the needs of really poor people. Jesus Christ always identified himself with the poor. In my own Congregation – the Order of the Jesuits – we took a decision at our last General Congregation to make what we've called a preferential option for the poor. This means that when we're considering new ventures we should ask ourselves, 'Is this going to be of service to the poorest people in the community, to the most oppressed? Is it going to bring them justice, is it going to bring them a better life?'

This speaks a lot to me because over the past three years I've been working in El Salvador with refugees and displaced people. People who have lost absolutely everything. I've felt very privileged to be able to work with them, and often I've thought of these words of Gandhi while I've been doing that work.

On his faith in God

I was working in El Salvador with people who have really suffered in a way in which perhaps here it's hard to imagine. Not only have they lost their possessions, but many of them have seen their mothers or fathers, their husbands or wives or their children, not only killed but tortured in front of their eyes. Yet those people themselves never lost their faith in God's goodness.

Many, many times I felt angry and rebellious. 'How can God permit such things? How can God exist if such things are going on?' I would ask myself, and then I would reflect, 'What right have I to say that when these people themselves have still preserved a very profound faith.' My faith was strengthened by them.

On his ministry

I studied Economics at the London School of Economics and my idea all the time was to see what the church could do to implement its social teaching, as we used to call it in those days. In other words, how the church could show a concern for the poor which goes beyond mere almsgiving, which tries to help them right the injustices in society. So during my studies, I asked permission to do my theology in a part of the Third World, in a poor country, and I was given that permission. I went to study my theology in Mexico and was ordained priest in Mexico City. During my three years there I was able to work in one of the slum *barrios*, or areas, of Mexico City and it was that experience that showed me that this was the work I hoped to be able to do for the rest of my life.

71

Extract from a letter written to Pandit Nehru by Mahatma Gandhi (1869–1948)

I will give you a talisman. Whenever you are in doubt, or when the self becomes too much with you, apply the following test. Recall the face of the poorest and weakest man whom you may have seen and ask yourself if the step you contemplate is going to be of any use to him. Will he gain anything by it? Will it restore him to control over his own life and destiny? In other words, will it lead to fulfilment for the hungry and spiritually starving millions? Then, you will find your doubts and your self melting away.

•

THE REVEREND WILLIAM R. DAVIES, President, Methodist Conference, 1987–88

On his conversion

It isn't that I didn't attend church when I was a youngster; I did. I attended Sunday School as anybody else did. I was made a church member when I was thirteen. But for a while I left the church after that. I suppose what I would say is that I understood what was being taught me with my head, but it hadn't really reached my heart. Having left the church, some four years later I went back again and was invited to attend a mission which was being conducted by theological students. I went to these meetings each night. The mission was in Blackpool where I was born. Then, one night after the beach mission meeting, on 19 July 1949, I went to a service in Chapel Street Methodist Church and there was a man preaching, George Allen who was a tutor at Cliff College. A saint of God he was, and he radiated Christianity. I can't remember what he preached about but I remember feeling that whatever it is that this man has I want it, and when they made an appeal for commitment at the end of the meeting I responded.

I suppose what happened there was that there was a resolution of an inner conflict that had been going on in me as to whether God was real or whether he wasn't, whether Jesus was alive or whether he wasn't, all this kind of thing. That night the conflict was resolved and all I can say is that it was a sort of liberating experience. I felt at peace. I felt a sense of joy, it was almost like walking on air, but inwardly, deeply I believed that what Jesus came to teach and say and do were true.

Before that I wasn't aware of being a deep-dyed sinner, but I think one can be bound without knowing it and what happened on that particular occasion, looking back, was that the liberty I experienced was from some sort of bondage, but it was bondage to self. Not that I'm perfect now, I would have you understand.

Twenty-one years later I had another crisis experience and it was at a time when I was going through a very hard, dry, barren period, when I was clinging on to the faith, and on this occasion I believe I experienced a touch of the Holy Spirit . . . a touch of the Spirit which renewed. On this occasion there was a sense of liberty, of being bound then and free now.

On his prayer

It's one of my favourite verses of Charles Wesley. We used to sing it at Sunday School and at youth club. We used to call it the Methodist National Anthem at the church where I was brought up. I use it fairly frequently in services that I conduct, probably more frequently than most.

Prayer by Charles Wesley (1707–88)

Long my imprisoned spirit lay
Fast bound in sin and nature's night;
Thine eye diffused a quickening ray –
I woke, the dungeon flamed with light;
My chains fell off, my heart was free,
I rose, went forth, and followed thee.

•

DR ABDEL HALEEM, Lecturer in Arabic at the School of Oriental and African Studies, London University

On the family

I grew up in Egypt, in a society which from the very earliest years teaches its children that marriage and family life are the best sort of relationship. At the birthday feast for a young man, or even a young boy, we would say, 'Many Happy Returns, and soon you will have your wife within your embrace.' We would say to a mother, 'Many Happy Returns and soon your daughter will be happily married . . . next year your daughter will be happily married.'

Then Islam teaches us that being married and having a spouse – a husband or a wife – is one of the great blessings of God. As the Koran says, 'He created for you, from within yourselves, spouses to find comfort in you and he established between you love and care.' These are signs for people to reflect upon.

This emphasis and approach helps people when they are married and in difficulties to try reconciliation and if it happens that the marriage breaks up, they immediately begin to think of getting married again.

On prayer

In Islam it's recommended that most prayers should be said in congregation. In fact, it is recommended that all prayers should be in congregation and congregation means more than one person. The best congregation to have is a family one in which the father and mother can lead the prayers and thus teach the children the prayers and bring them up in an atmosphere of prayer.

On his chosen prayer

The prayer tells us that parents should set a good example for their offspring so that they may become righteous. It is the duty of the parents to set a good example and the Koran enjoins the children to follow the good example set for them. Righteousness means being good and following decent and proper ways according to religion. The Koran tells us that when the parents set a good example and the children follow it, they will all be joined together in Paradise. This is important because what better company could we have in paradise but our own children and grandchildren. It's a great company to wish for. Paradise we hope will be a family paradise for those who set a good example and those who follow the right example.

Prayer from the Koran

Lord, grant us through our spouses and through our offspring peace and contentment, and make us a worthy example for the righteous.

•

ROBERT WHITE, Irish-American tenor

On his chosen prayer

It's a prayer that I remember from childhood. My mother used to say it to me all the time and my father used to sing it. It seemed to be asking for just enough to enable me to deal with whatever would occur in my life for the next twenty-four hours.

I sometimes find it very difficult to deal with life in a way which really copes with each day at a time. I can cope with difficulties, with problems which arise when some project or somebody is giving me a hard time. I deal with these in a straightforward way – so this has to be done, then I do it. But I find that I fret about just how I'm going to get through this week, these few days, sometimes these few hours. I worry and get frustrated over things which I have or haven't done, or which somebody else has done or not done. Then, I think of the words of this prayer and I find it helps to put things in the proper light.

I think it's because of the music which I associate with the prayer, because of the fact that my father always sang it, that it's remained a strong influence on me since my childhood, through adolescence to the present time. The music never allows the power of the prayer to weaken. I feel that because it's a song to me, I never felt that it was just a part of my parents, and therefore part of a package which every youth wants to reject after a time. No, I feel that these words come from something beyond my parents, that the truths that they tell are beyond family.

On sin and prayer

I'm not overly preoccupied by sin. It's something which we all have to cope with in our lives in our own ways, we have to deal with it. Obviously to be decent with one another is the most important thing that we can all keep striving for.

I can't say I pray every day. I don't. I do have at the back of my mind though an aspiration to do something in my life each day which will get me beyond the impediments in my thinking, will focus me on things beyond my immediate sadness, or mood. This prayer song helps me in this way to focus on this thing which is beyond and yet here.

The prayer speaks about sacraments and to me the sacraments signify peace and forgiveness. If you can find the blessing within your own soul of gratefulness for being alive, while you're here, and not spend the time griping about the fact of how awful it is to be here, I think this is terribly important. I always say to gripers, 'Think of the alternative. If you're not here, then life is gone.' I'd rather be here while I'm here.

From *Just for Today* by Sybil F. Partridge

Lord,
For tomorrow and its needs,
I do not pray,
Keep me, my God,
From stain of sin,
Just for today.
Let me both
Diligently work,
And duly pray,
And,
If today my tide of life should ebb away,
Give me, sweet Lord,
Thy sacraments divine,
So, for tomorrow and its needs,
I do not pray,
But keep me, guide and love me,
Lord,
Just for today.

•

THE REVEREND SISTER DENZIL, Guest Sister in the Anglican Community of St Andrew, west London

On maintaining a daily prayer habit

I've been thinking a lot about this lately because some of us have recently made an eight-day retreat in the House. It was wonderful, one had a long time for prayer. In a busy day it is so difficult, and I find that unless I get my prayer done early in the day, I've had it.

On her chosen prayer

The thing that attracts me to a particular prayer is if it uses the sort of language that sounds as if it's including everybody – men, women and children. Some of our language in the church seems as if it excludes women. It doesn't, it uses the word 'man' to cover all humankind; but some women find this exclusivity hurtful and I'm beginning to feel very sensitive about this too. So I look for inclusive language with regards to men and women, but also with regard to including the cross-section of people in society, particularly the people that Jesus seemed specially concerned with – the poor, the underprivileged, the homeless and ill-housed, the unemployed, the sick, the dying and so on.

The prayer I've chosen is written by a friend, a friend who I haven't seen for a long time, Jim Cotter. It's a prayer which includes people on the fringes of society, people such as Morris and Tom. They put some money in my Christian Aid tin one night when I was feeling very discouraged. I was coming home tired and they saw me go past with the tin and out of their poverty they put some coins in it. So for me it's a prayer for Morris and Tom and all the other people like them. It's also for my Community, my family, friends and my parish.

I think perhaps the best prayer is prayer without words, but that wouldn't really work on radio.

From *Prayer in the day* by Jim Cotter

Dear God, our Creator, beloved Companion and Guide upon
    the way, Eternal Spirit within us and beyond us,
Let us honour your name in lives of costly giving love,
Let us show that we, and all whom we meet, deserve dignity and
    respect, for they are your dwelling-place and your home.

Let us share in action your deep desire for justice and peace
  among the peoples of the world,
Let us share our bread with one another, the bread that you
  have shared with us,
Let us in the spirit of your forgiving us make friends with those
  we've hurt and failed to love,
Let us overcome our trials and temptations, our suffering and
  dying in the strength and courage with which you overcame
  them too,
Let us, in your love, free the world from evil, transforming
  despair into hope,
For the whole universe is yours and you invite us
To be partners in the work of your creating.
Amen.

●

JOHN WHITNEY, Director-General of the Independent Broadcasting Authority

On prayer

My earliest recollections are of my mother inviting me, nay,
bidding me to kneel at the side of my bed, put my hands
together and say the Lord's Prayer. Then we advanced from
that to prayers that she knew by heart and wanted to express
with me – prayers that related to the times as well, not just
prayers that existed for all time, but prayers that moved along
with the emphasis of events as they passed into our lives.

Perhaps because of this, I've always been aware of prayers as
a reflection of the times. They're very much a living thing with
us and always have been.

On his chosen prayer

I can remember it being read to me with the aid of a hurricane
lamp, an oil lamp. It was at a time when we had just moved into
our house and we hadn't yet got any electricity in. The prayer
enlarged my mind considerably. It made me realise that
although we had a temporary hardship of no electricity, there
were others in the world who have greater hardships. It's so
easy to go through one's day thinking ahead on the problems
one has to face without recognising that these problems are but

a tiny drop in an enormous ocean of problem and challenge. This prayer speaks, as we Quakers say, very much to my condition.

The thoughts in the prayer occur to me mostly in the mornings when I look at my diary for the day, or for the week, as I do normally on a Sunday and I see ahead of me all sorts of what I might consider to be precipices and rocks to climb, shoals to skirt and crevasses not to fall down. I wonder at the start of the week, just how I'm going to get through the coming days, then I think of this prayer and it puts everything into perspective. It shows me that all the things that I'm going to do are very very small compared with the very real needs of mankind. It acts as a very very good leveller to me, and that's what I need at the start of a day or a week.

The prayer also reminds me that we're very much one world. It pulls no punches, it speaks entirely to the spirit and it enjoins us all actively to challenge our own recognition of the wrongs in the world, and do something about it, not just sit and talk about it.

Prayer from *God of a Hundred Names*, collected and arranged by Barbara Green and Victor Gollancz

Let us never forget, O Lord,
The innocent victims of man's inhumanity to man,
The millions who were destroyed in the gas chambers
And in the holocaust of Hiroshima and Nagasaki,
And the few who survived, scarred in mind or body;
The uncounted numbers all over the earth
Who will never have enough to eat
And who, through poverty or ignorance,
Must watch their children die of hunger;
The lepers and the cripples and the countless others
Who live out their lives
In illness or disease for which they are given no relief;
All who suffer, because of their race or their creed,
Or the colour of their skins;
And all the children who, in their weakness,
Are torn from their parents
And robbed of the loving care which is their birthright.
Help us, as we go unheedingly about our daily lives,
To remember those who silently call on us,

And to remember also that
'Though the need of those in distress is so vast
And of such an infinite complexity,
It is by the steadfast effort of individuals
That it must be conquered.

•

NIGEL FORDE, poet, broadcaster and director of the Christian theatre company Riding Lights

On John Donne's poetry

We studied some Elizabethan poetry just for fun when we were doing 'A' levels at school, and I'd never come across anything quite so rich and rare before. There's something very purple about it – not in the sense that one talks about purple passages, but it was rich and deep and velvety and I loved it. This particular poem I first heard in a musical setting by Pelham Humphrey, on a record; and the music was so wonderful and fitted the words so perfectly that I had to read it again afterwards. I've loved it ever since.

On sin

I think one ought to have a proper regard for sin and repentance. The basis of prayer has got to be repentance, at least for me. I don't like shopping lists: 'God bless Auntie and God bless Granny and God bless so and so.' I think the thing on which one's relationship with God either starts or founders is to do with sin and repentance and this is so beautifully phrased and so applicable to Donne himself because he uses his name in this poem as a pun when he says, 'Thou hast done, and thou hast not done.' But at the same time one can read it and think, 'Yes, this is me as well, I have these problems and I have these fears.' I suppose most of our sins are sins of omission rather than sins of commission.

On God

The more you get to know about God, the more you get to know him, the closer you get, the further away you realise you are. That's the crux of the matter. Anything you say about God is only partially true, is only a tiny facet of a tiny facet.

But since the Bible uses the expression 'Father' so often, it seems to me that that's the easiest way in. Even though he's not really just a father, there's something about my relationship with God that the word father really pictures so that I can understand.

On forgiveness

It must be a wiping of the slate. If you like, it's a moral pretence that something hasn't happened. You know it has happened, but for all moral and ethical purposes you can say it doesn't matter: that's done and finished with and we won't think about it any more. That's something quite hard to do because the taste of it lingers on and it's as if you have to wash your mouth out. In this way I think repentance is the washing out of the mouth and accepting forgiveness is actually assuming that the taste isn't going to come back again.

Hymn to God the Father
John Donne (1573–1631)

Wilt thou forgive that sinne where I begunne,
Which was my sin, though it were done before?
Wilt thou forgive that sin through which I runne
And do run still: though still I do deplore?
When thou hast done, thou hast not done,
For, I have more.

Wilt thou forgive that sinne which I have wonne
Others to sinne? and, made my sinne their doore?
Wilt thou forgive that sinne which I did shunne
A year, or two: but wallowed in, a score?
When thou hast done, thou hast not done,
For I have more.

I have a sinne of fear, that when I have spunne
My last thred, I shall perish on the shore;
But sweare by thy selfe, that at my death thy sonne
Shall shine as he shines now, and heretofore;
And, having done that, Thou hast done,
I feare no more.

•

RABBI NORMAN SOLOMON, Director of the Centre for the Study of Judaism and Jewish/Christian Relations, Selly Oak Colleges, Birmingham

On prayer

There are times when prayer is a nuisance, I don't feel like it. There are other times when it expresses something very deep within me, and when I want to formulate spontaneous prayer as well. I think it's because of this that I appreciate the value of the usual traditional orthodox system in Judaism which is that there are regular fixed prayers plus an encouragement to adding spontaneous prayers. I think having the regular fixed prayers is a little bit like an athlete who's training. He's not going to win the race every day, he's not in that sort of condition, but he keeps training. If he stops training then he'll fall back. That's what happens with prayer. There are times when it's a struggle to keep on praying, you do it simply out of inertia. It's a habit, you do it because you did it the day before. But the habit's a good thing because when the emotional experience comes, you've got the words ready. You're in position like the athlete who's then ready to win the race and you know how to do it.

On the Torah

The word Torah is almost a word for religion – everything in the faith, belief, way of life, teaching, instruction, the whole thing. So when the prayer says 'Open my heart to thy Torah', it's asking to be able to go in the way that God wants. That's the way you get out of your stress. Your stress tries to push you in one direction, to hit against people, for instance. To open your heart to the Torah means to have your mind – for the word heart there really means mind – focused on the things that really matter, to have a right sense of values, not just a personal concern in your own fight and struggle.

On his chosen prayer

Once I was really in a bit of trouble and therefore noticing the words of prayers and this one got me. It just seemed to speak into the situation I was in. I was under a lot of pressure, people were attacking me for something or other and the natural instinct I suppose is to hit out and say horrible things back, but this prayer had the effect of releasing me from wanting to do that. I wasn't giving in, I wasn't changing my mind about the particular thing, but it gave me the strength to accept the blows that were coming from outside.

The prayer urges: Don't be selfish, don't be self-centred. Your soul should be as dust, the prayer says, in the sense that the attacks that people make should not disturb you inwardly. You'll react in a balanced and proper manner to them, but you'll not be carried away.

Prayer attributed in Babylonian Talmud Berakhot 7a to Mar the son of Ravina, a Babylonian rabbi of the early fourth century

O my God,
Guard my tongue from evil
And my lips from speaking guile.
To such as curse me,
Let my soul be dumb.
Yea, let my soul be unto all as the dust.
Open my heart to thy Torah
And let my soul pursue thy commandments.

•

HIS EMINENCE, CARDINAL BASIL HUME, Archbishop of Westminster

On first memories of Easter

My main memory is going off to church with the family – the five of us with our mother – and coming back for breakfast which, inevitably, on Easter Sunday would be boiled eggs. And I have very early memories of those coloured eggs. The coloured eggs were a special treat and underlined for us in the family that Easter Sunday was a special day. I think it's so important in families to underline the special days by something that you remember and the coloured eggs were my first way of remembering what Easter was. Only gradually did I discover the real meaning of Easter.

Easter Sunday was also important because we were allowed to eat sweets again. We didn't give up sweets voluntarily during Lent – that was imposed from on high by Mama.

On looking forward to Easter now

It's the wonderful ceremonies in the cathedral, the glorious prayers that we say, the music. There's a kind of atmosphere which has at its heart – *hope*. Hope is the great Easter gift. The gift of knowing that whatever life is like, whether we're suffering, whether we're sick, whatever we're living through – there is hope.

It's the death of the Lord followed by his resurrection, and so with us, all those things that are daily little deaths, they will have already within them a resurrection to a new life, to a new hope.

On his chosen prayer psalm

This is a psalm that I say often. It expresses very beautifully the longing of the soul, the longing of a person for God. It's one of those prayers that are prayed early on Easter Sunday morning by all those who are praying the special prayer of the church – the psalms.

On Good Friday we think of the Passion of our Lord. He lay on the Cross and he prayed Psalm 21, he said, 'My God, My God, why hast thou forsaken me?' He'd been abandoned by his friends and he went through that strange experience of feeling that he'd been abandoned by his Father. And so many people in our society do feel abandoned, they're marginalised for one reason or the other and they don't see any meaning to their lives, any purpose to their lives, so they even feel abandoned by God, and that's the terrible cry, 'Why hast thou forsaken me?' But this psalm (Psalm 63) starts with the words, 'O God, you are my God, for thee I yearn,' so the despairing soul is longing for God to come and give it meaning, give it purpose, give it love.

From Psalm 63

O God, you are my God, for you I long,
For you my soul is thirsty;
My body pines for you,
Like a dry, weary land without water.
So I gaze on you in the sanctuary,
To see your strength and your glory.
For your love is better than life,

My lips will speak your praise.
So I will bless you all my life;
In your name I will lift up my hands.
My soul shall be filled as with a banquet
My mouth shall praise you with joy.

•

RACHEL TRICKETT, Principal, St Hugh's College, Oxford

On her chosen prayer

It's a hymn I've always loved, particularly because of the image of the flame. The flame seems to me to be tremendously important as an image in religious thought and feeling – the flame of inspiration, the flame of love. The picture that it brings to my mind is of a lamp, or a candle, even a taper.

It's such a common image for inspiration in poetry. In one of the psalms the psalmist says, 'while I was thus musing the fire kindled'. I think it's that feeling of the fire kindling that Wesley wanted to convey in this hymn. We see this in the Old Testament as well as in the New, this idea of the flame burning for inspiration; Isaiah's coal, for instance, putting burning coal on the lips in order to release the inspiration.

On prayer

I suppose like most busy people the truth is that prayer has to take different forms in my life. To me the subject I taught here before I became Principal, and still teach, English Literature, is in its poetry at least a form of celebration of the divine in life for me. This would be so even in poetry that's secular, that isn't sacred like Wesley's hymn.

The sense of enjoyment in its deepest sense is very important to me spiritually. I know enjoyment is a non-spiritual feeling as well, but it does seem to me that to enjoy God forever, as the old catechism used to say, is in a sense prepared for by enjoying, as purely as we can, the beauty, the delight of this life. The sense of wonder is so important to me, the sense of wonder which anyone who leads a life which mercifully and happily is connected with art must be aware of, a sense of wonder which comprehends the whole of experience. The lack of this sense of wonder seems to me to be one of the basic sadnesses in modern society. There seems to be no outlet for wonder; less and less in the church, so that more and more people turn to superstitious, occult manifestations which are a sort of disease of the sense of wonder.

Prayer written by Charles Wesley (1707–88) as a hymn

O thou who camest from above,
The pure celestial fire to impart,
Kindle a flame of sacred love
On the mean altar of my heart.

There let it for thy glory burn
With inextinguishable blaze,
And trembling to its source return
In humble prayer, and fervent praise.

•

SIR COLIN DAVIS, Musical Director of the Bavarian Radio Symphony Orchestra, Musical Director, Royal Opera House, Covent Garden, 1971–86

On music and poetry

I think that what we get out of music is probably irrational, and I think that what we pray for is irrational, but I think that there's a positive side to being irrational and music and prayer belong to that side. There's also a very evil side to being irrational which we can see around us the whole time, but the positive irrationality which we might call the power of imagination, that is the greatest transforming influence which we have.

On achieving harmony in our nature

I think that creativity is the best way to do this and music is a wonderful way because when music begins you have to cease talking. If I may be completely heretical, I'm not sure that in the beginning was the word. I think in the beginning were the notes and I think that the devil fell and he stole from God this secret lexicon of words and spread these words about . . . you can't quarrel if you don't speak.

It is therefore the task of poets to rescue the words and put them back where they belong. Of course in the old days in Ireland, as Yeats never stops telling us, the poets were the priests. Any creativity is a positive use of time.

On human nature and on his chosen verse by John Donne

There's much of Donne which touches the mortal as well as the immortal. I mean, if ever there was a more beautiful schizophrenic than Donne I don't know one, but he was honest, he admitted at least two sides to himself. I think that our problem is that we have so many sides to ourselves that to get all these aspects of our nature into a kind of harmony takes more than one lifetime.

There's a very beautiful verse by Donne which he wrote when he was ill, and of course when one is very ill one must have the thought that this may very well be one's last illness. He talks as though he is in the Green Room before he is going on to a concert and he is tuning his violin which of course is his symbol for our attempts to draw all the strands of our nature together.

Hymn to my God in my Sickness
John Donne (1573–1631)

Since I am coming to that Holy room,
Where, with thy Quire of Saints for evermore,
I shall be made thy Music; as I come
I tune the Instrument here at the door,
And what I must do then, think here before.

•

THE MOST REVEREND DESMOND TUTU,
Archbishop of Cape Town

On his chosen prayer

You look at the Cross and you think of Good Friday and you say nothing could have been more hopeless than Good Friday, and then Easter happens and everything is let loose and God's power is available. The Prayer of St Francis for me articulates this wonderful belief that because of the Resurrection all of us for ever must be prisoners of hope.

You speak too about the fact that nothing and nobody is irredeemable, and in the prayer one is seen as a fellow worker with God, helping God in his enterprise to turn the ugliness of the world into the beauty of his kingdom, the hatreds into friendliness, and the prayer speaks right at the end about how we die and it is in dying that we rise to life eternal.

How does one become this fellow worker with God, how does one empty oneself? I realise more and more just how much I depend on other people and that everything about a Christian really is corporate and that in many ways it doesn't matter if one, as it were, fails, others make up for it, others uphold you. Sometimes you make good and your 'success' permeates the whole body. I think it is a lifetime business, this trying to empty oneself and therefore to reflect the character of God as revealed in our Lord Jesus Christ.

Mercifully God does not give up on anybody. God always sees not the caterpillar, but the butterfly all of us have it in us to become, and this is true even in instances when God's power somehow seems to be limited by our limitations. We have an extraordinary God who although all-powerful, omnipotent, is willing to risk the success of his enterprise to transfigure the world by enlisting us as his partners. It's quite incredible, it's staggering, and God doesn't say when we have failed, 'Oh, good riddance,' as it were, 'of bad rubbish,' and wash his hands of us. He dusts us off and says, 'Have another go.'

The prayer of St Francis of Assisi (1181–1226)

O Lord, make me an instrument of thy peace.
Where there is hatred, let us sow love,
Where there is injury, pardon;
Where there is doubt, faith;
Where there is despair, hope;
Where there is darkness, light;
Where there is sadness, joy.
O divine Master, Grant that we may not so much seek
To be consoled, as to console,
To be understood, as to understand,
To be loved, as to love,
For it is in giving that we receive;
It is in pardoning that we are pardoned,
And it is in dying that we are born to eternal life.   Amen.

PENELOPE ECKERSLEY, retreat director and writer on spirituality

On the attraction to her of her chosen meditation

The words reflected the sense that within the ordinary you can discover the divine. It was something I was working on with groups in retreat and it's always nice to find a quotation which is tight and close to what you're trying to say.

I think that God is within nature. I think God is within all matter. Most of the time we're far too busy rushing about the world at a great pace, bothering about the surface of things, and in order to get below the surface we need to do something, we need to make a move ourselves.

We're just beginning to return to this kind of understanding of God in our appreciation of Celtic spirituality. They were very close to the natural world in which they lived and the sense not that you have to placate the Gods of the storm and the sea, but that within these forces you discover God. I think this sort of understanding is helping a lot of people who aren't prepared to take on board the intellectual framework of Christian belief.

On nature

Nature is life, it's like any other aspect of life. It has its cruel side and its dark side. In life or relationships it's sometimes very difficult to have a sense of trust. So with nature. But I think these times are also good tests of the quality of our belief or our sense of trust, which is a kind of faith in what's behind it all . . . what's behind the movements in nature, hurricanes, earthquakes, and what's behind the movements within relationships. I don't think these are really very different.

Nothing grows and changes without a certain amount of struggle and very often pain and difficulty. That process is going on at every level within creation.

On God

I draw back from using words which imply that God as Creator is a sort of person. I think God, as Teilhard de Chardin said, 'is continual discovery, continuous growth', and continues to give light . . . enlightenment.

From the Gospel of Thomas

Cleave a piece of wood, I am there.
Lift up the stone, and you will find me.

•

BRIAN BOOBBYER, English rugby international in the early 1950s

On his chosen meditation

The thing I always like about the letters of St Paul is that everything he says is absolutely all out, no punches spared. He starts this particular passage by saying, 'Commit your life to God.' There's no half measures about it. But he also goes on to say, 'Don't let the world around you squeeze you into its own mould,' and it's exactly what the world so easily does. Another translation, for instance, says, 'Do not conform to this world, but be ye transformed.' The great question that people ask is just how they can go about being transformed.

I remember when I was a student at Oxford, another sportsman who was a good friend of mine one day challenged me. He said, 'Why don't you spend time listening to God?' I was a bit embarrassed, as the English often are when deep things are mentioned, but I went away and thought about it. The following day I went back to my room and spent ten minutes in quiet, not looking at the glamorous sportsman I often thought I was, but looking at the underneath: the hopes, fears, and weaknesses; in fact the truth about myself. These ten minutes became a sort of discipline. My listening time became twenty minutes and eventually half an hour. I used to set an alarm clock to help the process because if I wasn't going to let the world around me squeeze me into its mould, I had to make the sacrifice of time, the sacrifice that enables God to get through to me.

That was the challenge that was put to me then, and I've kept up the practice of a quiet time ever since. I find that I can get this time to listen in the early morning and, as Paul goes on to suggest, I find in the listening, something of the will of God for me for the day: what I may be able to do for someone – perhaps to be a friend to somebody, even maybe get an inspired thought that could be a strategy for a particular situation baffling me.

To help me to listen I read a passage from the Bible, a passage which stimulates my mind. I'm not always at my most alert in the morning so the passage helps to get the brain working. I pray. There's not really a set pattern. What's important is that I give the time. I write down my thoughts – I'm not presuming that everything that comes into my mind comes from God, but I'm sure that some of the thoughts do. I know that it's my own very best, the result of asking God to speak to me. That's the important thing . . . asking for guidance and listening for it in the early morning. Then I leave my room, full of hope about people and hope for the world.

On God

I grew up as a Christian and in a Christian environment, so when I think about God, I think of Jesus Christ, and a Jesus Christ who is very personal. In a way Jesus Christ is my very best friend and it's very difficult, quite honestly, to put my feelings or my experience of him into words. He's there, I can talk to him, he talks to me, it's a very personal thing. But we're all at different stages. Some of us have a very thin thread of God and some of us have a big one, but we can all start moving along this difficult road to getting to know God, by listening to him.

Epistle of Paul to the Romans, Chapter 12, verses 1 and 2

With eyes wide open to the mercies of God I beg you, my brothers, as an act of intelligent worship, to give him your bodies as a living sacrifice, consecrated to him, and acceptable by him. Don't let the world around you squeeze you into its own mould: but let God remake you, so that your whole attitude of mind is changed. Thus you will prove in practice that the will of God is good, acceptable to him, and perfect.

●

THE RIGHT REVEREND CRISPIAN HOLLIS,
Auxiliary Bishop of Birmingham based in Oxford

On the importance to him of personal prayer

I think it's changed and it's varied from time to time, from
stage to stage in my life. To start with you get used to the
formal prayers, the familiar prayers of the church which we
learn at our mother's knees, as it were. But gradually we come
to realise that God's calling us into something very personal,
something that demands a personal response and that's prayer.
Prayer takes time, it needs a lot of silence and a lot of
generosity. I get silence in the early morning. That's my time.
I'm one of those people who doesn't mind getting up first thing
in the morning, so that's my time for prayer.

On his chosen prayer

I was educated by the Jesuit Fathers at Stonyhurst College in
Lancashire and they've been a great influence in my life. The
founder of the Jesuits was a saint called St Ignatius of Loyola.
One of his great gifts to the church was a thing called The
Spiritual Exercises which is really a thirty-day retreat. I've
never done it, I haven't got the time to do a thirty-day retreat
and I'm not sure I'd be very good at doing thirty days in
silence, but at the end of the fourth week of the retreat, he
produces a Contemplation for Obtaining Love. In that Contemplation he has a particular prayer which is very special to
me and which I say from day to day. I don't say I live up to it
but it's a statement of intent, it's what I'd like to make of my
life.

It's a reflection of what God has given me freely and
absolutely and it's an attempt, however poor, by me, to
respond to that with the giving of myself in return. In theory
that's quite easy but in practice it means giving myself to
people and that can be difficult or easy according to how
difficult or easy people are.

An important thing in the prayer, for me, is what it says
about memories. It asks God to receive my memories, to take
them from me. We can live a lot in our memories, and
memories can be good, and memories can be bad. Sometimes
we get haunted by bad memories either of failures in our own
lives or unpleasant things that have happened to us. These

memories aren't positive, they drag us down. The prayer is very much one for the healing of memories. It reminds me of how much I've been forgiven for the sins I've committed and that the Lord says, 'Give me your memories, and I will look after them. You needn't worry about them.'

Prayer from a Contemplation for Obtaining Love, taken from the Spiritual Exercises of St Ignatius of Loyola

Take, O Lord, and receive
All my liberty, my memory, my understanding
And all my will,
Whatever I have or possess.
You have given all these things to me.
To you, O Lord, I restore them.
They are yours,
Dispose of them according to your will.
Give me your love and your grace
For this is enough for me.

•

NARINDER SINGH BIRDI, an engineer and teacher at the Sikh Temple Ramgarhia Sabha, Southall, London

On his chosen prayer

The prayer comes from the Holy Book of the Sikhs, the *Granth Sahib*. The book says that people call God by different names but that God is always the same, the One Creator All Almighty, and you can call him by any name you love to choose. In fact the book teaches me to respect other people's religions, feelings, beliefs and understandings, and to share my feelings with them.

The words of the prayer I've chosen are important to me because they're the words with which I start my day. They're words that help me overcome problems and difficulties. When I see difficulties coming I say the words, 'The Lord and the Protector, the God Almighty has showered his grace on me and is protecting me at all times.'

Prayer is absolutely important to me. It's like my daily food, it's the food for my soul. I set aside time for prayer in the early morning and again when I come to work. As soon as I enter the building, I say this prayer so that I start my day and my work by remembering God. By saying the prayer I remember to do my best at work to contribute practically, physically and spiritually towards my work and towards helping my colleagues who work with me.

I feel that whatever sorrow, whatever happiness, whatever difficulties come our way, these are God's will and I have to abide by that will. To help me abide with that will, I choose the prayer and say it. God made me within his will as he wants me to be.

The Perfect Guru in this prayer is meant to be God, God the Teacher who teaches us everything. At the end of the prayer there is a mention of Nanak. Guru Nanak was the first Guru of the Sikhs and the Holy Light of God passed from Guru Nanak up to the 10th Guru, Guru Gobind Singh and was finally installed in the form of Word in the *Granth Sahib*. There's a wonderful sense of continuity.

Prayer, 'Tati Vau Na Lagayee', from the *Guru Granth Sahib*, the Holy Book of the Sikhs

Whoever is under the protection of God Almighty, hot wind blows not over them.

I am surrounded from all sides by the protection of the Lord, thus no pain disturbs me.

I try to follow the perfect Guru who has made me as he desired. He has passed me with the remedy of the Lord's name and I am with him now. I only remember one God Almighty.

The protector Lord has saved me and cured me of all my pains and sorrows.

Nanak says, 'The Lord has extended his grace to me therefore I have acquired the support of God Almighty.'

INDEX OF CONTRIBUTORS

INDEX OF FIRST LINES